GOOD OLD GRITS COOKBOOK

GOOD OLD GRITS COOKBOOK

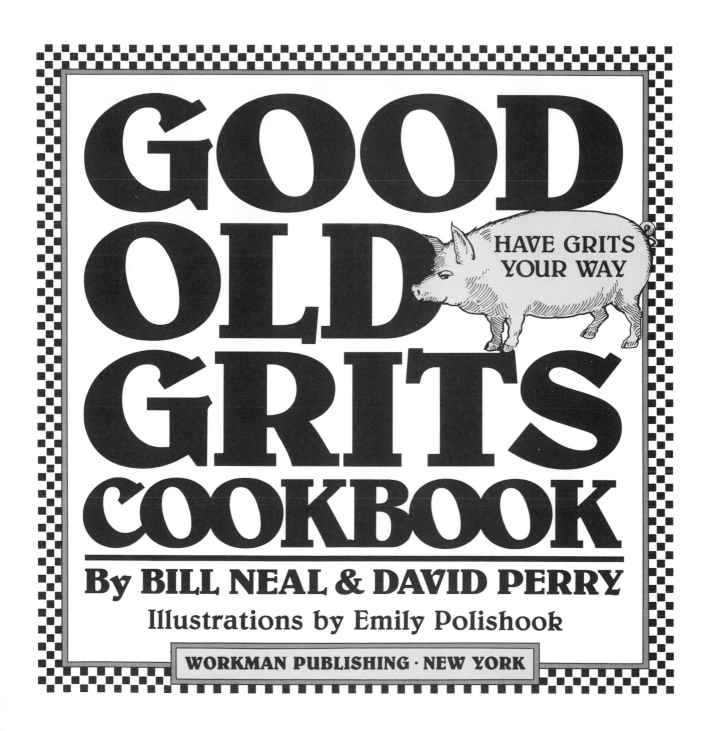

HAVE GRITS YOUR WAY

By BILL NEAL & DAVID PERRY

Illustrations by Emily Polishook

WORKMAN PUBLISHING · NEW YORK

Grits Pudding, Creamy Butterscotch Grits, and Luscious Peachy Grits Cheesecake used by permission
of Martha White Foods.
"Song to Grits" from *One Fell Soup* by Roy Blount, Jr., copyright © 1975 Roy Blount, Jr.; reprinted by
permission, Little, Brown and Company.

Library of Congress Cataloging-in-Publication Data

Neal, Bill.
Good old grits cookbook : have grits your way / by Bill Neal and David Perry.
p.   cm.
Includes index.
ISBN 0-89480-865-6 (pbk.)   ISBN 1-56305-096-X
1. Cookery (Corn)   2. Grits.   I. Perry, David, 1947–   .
II. Title.
TX809.M2N43   1991
641.6'567—dc20   90-50946
                                                                                                                         CIP

Cover and book design by Lisa Hollander
Book illustrations by Emily Polishook

Workman Publishing Company, Inc.
708 Broadway
New York, NY 10003

Manufactured in the United States of America

First printing April 1991
10 9 8 7 6 5 4 3 2 1

ACKNOWLEDGMENTS

. . . . . .

We began this book with a few questions—Where did grits come from? Why do southerners eat them? Why do others not? Our attempts to answer those questions led us to supermarkets in Oakland and Amish food shops in Philadelphia. We inspected menus in roadside diners and uptown restaurants. We talked to food writers, folklorists, historians, and cooks from Charleston to Little Rock.

Our way was made easier by the work of some who had gone before us. John Egerton's many references to grits in his book *Southern Food: At Home, on the Road, in History* (1987) and his entry on the subject in the *Encyclopedia of Southern Culture* (1989) got us started in the right direction. Nicolas P. Hardeman's *Shucks, Shocks, and Hominy Blocks: Corn as a Way of Life in Pioneer America* (1981) is the source of much of our information on the growing and processing of corn in early America. Sam Bowers Hilliard's *Hog Meat and Hoecake: Food Supply in the Old South, 1840–1860* (1972) and Joe Gray Taylor's *Eating, Drinking, and Visiting in the South: An Informal History* (1982) were invaluable resources. The writings of Roy Blount, Jr., on southern food and

southerners in general reminded us that our subject was grits and that a little levity would not be out of order.

Charles Parnell, who with his wife, Heidi, restored and now operates the Old Mill at Guilford in Oak Ridge, North Carolina, was a patient instructor in the ways of milling and the miller's art. We spent a delightful and absorbing day with Don Hatch, longtime brand manager for grits and other corn products for Quaker Oats, who must know more about the grits business than anyone alive. Linda Carman, of Martha White Foods, shared with us her own file of newspaper clips and other information on grits and saved us from many errors of fact.

We figure that between our two families we have eaten over 150 pounds of grits in these last two years as we have worked over and perfected the recipes in this book. Our children no longer ask whether a dish has grits in it. It is assumed. It is to them— Christine, Charles, Madeline, Elliott, and Matt—that we dedicate this book.

CONTENTS

. . . . . .

SONG TO GRITS

. . . . . .

When my mind's unsettled,
When I don't feel spruce,
When my nerves get frazzled,
When my flesh gets loose—

What knits
Me back together's grits.

Grits with gravy,
Grits with cheese.
Grits with bacon,
Grits with peas.
Grits with a minimum
Of two over-medium eggs
mixed in 'em: um!

Grits, grits, it's
Grits I sing—
Grits fits
In with anything.

Rich and poor, black and white,
Lutheran and Campbellite,
Jews and Southern Jesuits,
All acknowledge buttered grits.

Give me two hands, give me my wits,
Give me forty pounds of grits.

Grits at taps, grits at reveille.
I am into grits real heavily.

True grits,
More grits,
Fish, grits and collards.
Life is good where grits are swallered.

Grits
Sits
Right.

—ROY BLOUNT, JR.
One Fell Soup

SOUTHERN GOLD

· · · · · ·

At breakfast we had a big bowl of water-ground hominy grits that had simmered for an hour over a slow fire. We never missed having hominy and we never tired of it, we could eat it, and did eat it, every morning of every year, and we were never able to understand why people in the Middle West, in the corn country, did not eat hominy too. Hominy was such a good food, eaten with butter or with sliced tomatoes or with red gravy, and it was so cheap. We do not know what we would do in the South, white folks or black folks, if there were no hominy grits. We had red gravy in bowls and wide platters filled with thick slices of ham, smoked and cured and fried, and we had fried eggs right from the nests. We had pitcherfuls of rich milk that had been chilled overnight in the spring branch, and we had blackberry jam for the hot biscuits, and preserves made from the little clingstone peaches that grew wild on the terraces in the cotton patches and were sweeter than anything we ever cultivated in the orchards. We liked everything that was wild.

—BEN ROBERTSON
Red Hills and Cotton: An Upcountry Memory

INTRODUCTION

On every breakfast plate in the South there always appears a little white mound of food. Sometimes it's ignored. Sometimes insulted. But without it, the sun wouldn't come up, the crops wouldn't grow, and most of us would lose our drawl. It's grits.

Yes, we've heard that a few apostate southerners have shunned the morning call to grits. A gentleman (term loosely applied) from Dallas allowed in print that the best recipe for grits is to make them and throw them away. We have also suffered the irreverent allusions to wallpaper paste.

But true southerners approach this simple bowl of boiled corn with respect. Grits has what our mothers like to call stick-to-itiveness. Eat grits in the morning and you are steadied and ready to face the day. It's grits that carries us through work and play in the South. And it's the grits that have been on our plates for generations—all the way back to the Indians— that say this is America's first food.

More has been written about southern cooking than about any other American cuisine. Food experts have invaded the South, peeping into our pantries and rambling through our spice racks, looking for the secrets of

our good cooking. And they have come to the studied conclusion that the foundation of southern cooking is corn. It's the basis of our soups and chowders, Brunswick stew, fritters and pancakes, dodgers and ashcakes. We eat corn green, stewed, pickled, ground, fried, and baked.

Well, if corn is the foundation, corn grits is the mortar that holds it all together. By itself, grits is a pretty bland concoction. But nobody eats grits that way. Grits come with a little sausage, two eggs, biscuits, and red-eye gravy. Southern cooks beat grits up with eggs, grate in a little cheese, press in some garlic, and bake to make the grits casserole. Or they sauté some shrimp with bacon and scallions and serve it on a bed of cheese grits.

For reasons we have never been able to understand, the court of food opinion has not been kind to grits. We hear a lot more about the fine qualities of foods with much shorter pedigrees than grits. A few years ago, food writers went to great lengths to promote the virtues of polenta. Southerners recognize polenta as just another name for cornmeal mush. And where did it come from anyway? The Italians didn't even know about corn until the sixteenth century, when European explorers brought it back from the New World. Americans, Native Americans that is, had been eating grits for five thousand years by that time.

In all its long history, though, grits has

made only two public appearances outside the South. The first was when Jimmy Carter ascended to the presidency. (Remember "Grits and Fritz"?) Pundits proclaimed that the South had rejoined the nation, and grits in the White House was the proof. Suddenly grits were chic and served in swank Washington bistros and at lavish parties in New York's Central Park.

That era passed quickly, and perhaps mercifully, because humble grits doesn't wear the mantle of chic very well. The second grits renaissance began in the eighties and promises to be with us a lot longer. Food writers rediscovered the richness of American regional food, and imaginative chefs found grits a perfect medium for their creations.

A healthy portion of the credit for the second coming of grits must go to New Yorker (née Mississippian) Craig Claiborne, who never tires of serving grits to his guests and never missed a chance to pass along a good grits recipe to his readers in the *New York Times*. In 1985 Claiborne visited our Chapel Hill restaurant, Crook's Corner, and sampled shrimp and grits. He featured the recipe in a *Times* article and later in his book on southern cooking. Today it is our most popular dish. Last year we served over ten thousand plates of shrimp and grits.

WHAT'S IN A NAME?

If the first settlers had been French, they might have called the food **semoule de maïs** *(ground corn), adding class to the nomenclature and dollars to the price. Such euphemistic ploys have done wonders for goose liver, fish eggs, and snails.*
—JERRY DeLAUGHTER
American Way

The Indians who met the first Virginia colonists offered the newcomers steaming bowls of cracked grains of maize cooked into a kind of stew. They called it *ustatahamen*, thought to be the source of today's term "hominy." The word "grits" came with the settlers. Grits originally meant the bran and chaff that was left over from grinding Old World grains. By the sixteenth century, grits had come to mean any coarsely ground grain, especially oats.

Indian hominy was dried whole corn kernels boiled with lye to loosen the husk; it was often then dried and cracked. Here's the first recipe in English for hominy grits. It comes from John Smith, who valued corn above gold in his Virginia settlement. In 1629 he wrote, "Their servants commonly feed upon Milke Homini, which is bruized Indian corne pounded, and boiled thicke, and milke for the sauce."

The original name, hominy grits, still appears on the packages of grits sold by Quaker Oats and other companies, but the food has long since lost its connection to the old-fashioned lye soak process. Today it refers, generically, to corn grits, that is, dried corn that has been hulled and roughly ground.

In Charleston, just to confuse things further, "hominy" means simply "grits"—the dish cooked and ready to eat. Uncooked grits Charlestonians refer to as "grist." To quote from the Junior League of Charleston's *Charleston Receipts* cookbook, "Never call it 'Hominy Grits' / Or you will give Charlestonians fits! / When it comes from the mill, it's 'grist'; / After you cook it well, I wist, / You serve *'hominy'*!"

GRITS IS/GRITS ARE

Grammarians have written reams on the southern usage of the word grits. One question they never tire of trying to answer is "Is grits singular or plural?" Webster's says "noun plural, but singular or plural in construction." The *Oxford English Dictionary* is even less help. "In America, fine hominy is called grits," the learned dons declare, "and wheat prepared in the same way is likewise so designated." (Wheat grits? Not in the South.)

Richard Allin, of the *Arkansas Gazette*, comes down firmly on the side of the pluralists. "After pondering the situation, I can't think of many reasonable uses in the singular. Strange sounding beyond hope would be, 'This grits needs more butter' or 'Would you like another grits?' Maybe one could get by with, 'Grits is a common dish on the southern breakfast (and dinner, and supper) table.' But 'Have a grits on me' is nonsense. And 'grit' is meaningless."

Those who study actual usage, however, come away with a different notion. Stan Woodward dedicated a whole movie, called "It's Grits," to the question. He went around South Carolina pushing a hand-held camera in people's faces and asking, "Do you say 'Grits is?' or 'Grits are?'" About half his subjects were sure it was "grits is"; the rest were just as sold on "grits are."

The closest thing we have to a person-on-the-street survey occurred in the spring of 1990 at the World Grits Festival in St. George, South Carolina. Drew Jubera, of the *Atlanta Constitution*, asked several people for their innermost thoughts on the subject of grits. (We added the emphasis.) "Grits *is* wonderful," said Neil Bennett, of Bennett's Appliance Store. "Don't spit *'em* out, Fran," a spectator called to a participant in the "grits wearing" contest. "They [Yankees] love *it*," Virginia Norred said. "They just don't know how to cook *it*." "*They* gritty," said Candy Card, "and *they* got to have a little jelly and ketchup and salt." Putting sugar on grits "messes *it* up," said Judy Knight, of Columbia. "*They* taste like . . . like grits," affirmed Donald Stone, of Johnsonville, South Carolina.

If grammar follows usage, then maybe Webster's wasn't so far off after all. We say, use your ear. All southerners do. Anyway, who's to say you're wrong?'

ORIGINS

[Hominy blocks] were as much a part of the pioneer American scene as fireplaces and rain barrels. By the eighteenth century, every cabin and clearing had one or two of them. Sailors could sometimes tell when they were nearing the East Coast in a fog because of the "thump, thump, thump" of samp mills. And pioneers used these thudding contraptions like signal drums to communicate with each other. Southern planters, who forbade their slaves to have drums for fear of insurrection, were at times apprehensive that the blacks were beating signals among themselves with the ever-present hominy blocks.

—NICHOLAS P. HARDEMAN
Shucks, Shocks, and Hominy Blocks

Corn had supported Indian civilization for several thousand years by the time the Europeans arrived. Some botanists think that Indians in central Mexico domesticated the grain from a strain of wild corn. By the time of the European encounter with the New World, corn-based civilizations stretched from central Argentina to Maine. A party sent out by Columbus found the grain growing in Cuba and took news of their discovery back to Europe.

The Indians of the Eastern American woodlands lived in villages, the better to keep watch over their corn patches. The Virginia colonists adapted quickly to the ways of corn culture, copying unashamedly (and seldom crediting) the Indians' highly evolved methods for growing, harvesting, storing, and preparing corn. That first year they traded beads and trinkets with the Indians for enough grain to keep the colony from starvation. The next year they proudly claimed to have forty acres of corn under cultivation. By 1630 the colony was exporting grain to other colonies.

Westward settlement was in part a scramble for better corn lands. The great trans-Appalachian migration from New England and the Mid-Atlantic states led to the Midwest's corn belt. Southern expansion carried settlers across the Gulf states. We hear a lot about King Cotton, but acreage devoted to corn in the South was several times that given to cotton during the pioneer period.

Corn was an ideal crop for the early settlers because it grows in a variety of soils and climates, gives a good yield per acre (three to four times that of wheat), and stores well. Once corn has dried past the green corn stage, though, it must be husked and ground before it can be eaten. The Indians pounded their lye-soaked grains in a giant wooden mortar with a hand-held pestle. The settler usually worked with a "hominy block." It used a massive wooden mortar in the Indian fashion, but its pestle was a section of tree trunk suspended from an overhanging limb. Its advantage was a spring action in the grinding process.

Cracking corn in a hominy block was anything but efficient. The resulting grind included everything from meal-size particles to loose husks. Meal was sifted out, to be made into cornbread, mush, or any one of a number of other corn dishes. The larger particles that remained, after the husks were washed off, were the grits.

The second wave of settlers, following the path blazed by the pioneers, brought town builders and small businessmen, and one of the first businesses set up in every community was the grist mill. The miller used the power of falling water to turn the big wheel, which turned the grinding stones. It took two stones to grind grain, usually set one above the other. The miller poured whole corn into a hole in the middle of the upper stone, and as the grain worked its way out between the stones it was cracked and ground into a fine meal. The meal was then "bolted," or sifted. The finer screens yielded meal, while the larger meshes gave grits. The husk and other chaff were usually caught by the sifter and either added back to the meal or used for animal feed.

Because these mills ground the corn whole, the oily germ as well as the starchy endosperm, the resulting meal and grits were high in oil, vitamins, and flavor but did not keep well. Families ground only what they needed for the near future, and trips to the mill were frequent. The stone-ground grits today still retain this nutritional heritage. Store them in the freezer so they don't go rancid.

Our modern grits, commercially milled and neatly packaged and sitting on a supermarket shelf, seem far removed from the pioneer's hominy block. In the modern processing of grits, the hulls are loosened by soaking the kernels in water for several hours and are then pulled off by air suction. Then the kernel is broken down into several pieces in a "degerminator," and the germ and any remaining hull are removed. The remaining part of the kernel, the endosperm, is dried and then ground in a rolling mill. The finer pieces become cornmeal and the heavier pieces become grits.

In the supermarket, you are likely to encounter standard—or old-fashioned—grits, quick grits, and instant grits. During the milling quick grits are lightly steamed and lightly compressed so as to fracture the particles. The result is that quick grits cook in two to five minutes instead of the thirty to forty minutes recommended for standard grits. Concerning instant grits, the less said the better. Let's put it this way: If you like instant coffee, you're ready for instant grits.

Not just any corn will do for grits. Because of long-standing preferences, grits are usually white, made from white corn. (People in the South used to say that yellow corn was only good for the hogs.) White corn for grits and meal is grown in a few isolated pockets in the South, but the vast majority of the white corn crop is grown in a small area of southern Illinois and adjacent Missouri, under contract to Quaker Oats and other large millers. Grits lovers should pay special attention to weather conditions in that area. A drought or flood would severely threaten the supply of grits and white cornmeal.

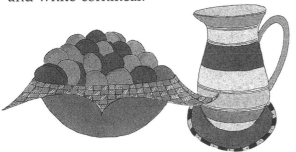

PRIDE OF THE SOUTH

Perhaps the most significant aspect of southern foodways is the persistence of food preferences once they were established. . . . The traditional southern foods have survived the settlement years, a civil war, and more than a century of time to become a frontier 'relic' in the midst of twentieth-century American life.

—SAM HILLIARD
Hogmeat and Hoecake

So why do southerners eat grits, while folks from other parts of the country don't? The easy answer, and perhaps the best answer, is that southerners eat grits because they always have. Corn was important in the early years in all of the seaboard colonies. Who has not heard the story of Squanto teaching the Pilgrims to fertilize their corn crops with alewives? We have even seen references to the making of hominy grits in New England in the seventeenth century. John Josselyn, in *New Englands Rarities Rediscovered* (1672), says, "They beat the corn in a mortar and sift the flower out of it: the remainder they call Homminey."

Southerners, though, held to the corn diet long after other parts of the country had gone on to wheat. For one thing, wheat didn't grow too well in the Deep South. And plantation owners, with slaves to feed and house and high overhead from their investment in land and equipment, were more interested in raising the dependable cash crops of tobacco and cotton than in some other food crop. Corn was grown everywhere in the South; it was so plentiful that it was not profitable to ship it very far.

Successive waves of immigrants brought new influences and preferences to the North. Not so in the South, where transportation remained primitive, and immigration was not nearly as much of a factor in population growth. Wheat had replaced corn as the grain of choice for human consumption in most parts of the North by the beginning of the nineteenth century; corn—and grits—remained dominant in the South.

And eat grits the southerners did, smothered in gravy, sliced and fried, mixed with sausage and eggs and baked, cooked into breads, whipped into delicate soufflés, and even topped with molasses or honey for a sort of dessert. Grits have completely permeated our ways of cooking and eating. Even for northerners, grits symbolize southern culture.

AREN'T YOU GLAD YOU EAT GRITS? DON'T YOU WISH EVERYBODY DID?

Not even the most ardent lover of grits would think of eating it alone. Basically it is an insipid mass, much like mashed potatoes. But add butter and salt or any one of the many tasty items found particularly in the South and you're on your way to a pleasant experience. The Southerner's devotion to grits is really meant for grits-and-gravy, grits-and-ham, grits-and-sausage, grits-and-eggs, grits-with-meat-and-cheese, and so on ad infinitum.

—TURNER CATLEDGE
New York Times

Southerners are not by nature selfish. So it's a puzzle to us why we have insisted for so long on keeping the attractions of grits a secret from the rest of the country. And there's no doubt that a lot of the responsibility for the mystification of grits is ours. How else to explain our pleasure at the bafflement grits causes northerners?*

In the past year we have talked to

---

*For the purposes of this book, we will use the standard southern definition of "northerner," that is, anyone not from the South. So if you are from Boston, Boise, or San Diego, you are a northerner.

hundreds of people about grits. And we have found that the world is not divided into those who eat grits and those who don't, as we had thought. It is divided into those who have eaten them all their lives and those who have eaten them only once.

It's a fact. Ask your friends. Practically everyone from the non-grits states has tried them. And they remember the experience, usually vividly.

Typically, their first and only encounter with grits takes place in some local diner in the Deep South, on a trip to Florida. The family stumbles in to breakfast after passing the night in a motel. They order full breakfasts, and when the plates arrive, alongside the bacon and eggs and biscuits is a mound of white stuff.

"What's that?" Dad asks the waitress.

"It's grits," she answers.

"What's grits?"

"I dunno. It's . . . just grits."

"Well, what do you do with it?"

"You eat it."

And having provided all the orientation she figures is needed, the waitress retires, leaving the family to figure out the rest. Mom picks up a bit on her fork and samples it. "It isn't bad," she pronounces. "Just try some."

One of the kids takes a bite. "Yecch! It tastes like library paste."

Dad decides it must be a sort of hot break-fast cereal, and he pours syrup on his, just like he does his oatmeal back home. It's not too good, but he doesn't admit it.

Mention grits to these folks years later, and memories of that morning in Valdosta, Georgia, come flooding back. Grits! Library paste. Yecch! The problem, of course, is that a mound of grits on a plate in a Georgia diner is strange food for someone not familiar with it. Maybe if the waitress had sat down in the booth with the family, she could have shown them how to eat grits.

"Y'all got your forks? Okay now, cut into one of the eggs and let the yellow run toward the grits. Fork up some of those grits. Now get you a piece of sausage on the end. Drag the whole thing through that yellow egg juice. Eat it.

"Wudn't that good? You got it now?"

So here we are, two southerners who come bearing grits, their legends, their lore, and now, the ways to cook and eat them. Grits are still a way of life in the South; they're a link to our fathers and mothers, and to generations lost. And they are a link to the natives, whose generosity is seldom acknowledged.

When the Indians offered bowls of boiled cracked corn to the first European settlers, they weren't just saying, "Eat this." The name some Indian groups gave to the grain, "maize," meant "that which sustains life."

They were offering a vision of the universe in which man, agriculture, religion, and the forces of nature were in beautiful harmony. Offering a bowl of grits was an invitation to share in their lifestyle.

No wonder Southerners still approach this simple dish with not a little reverence. It is a reminder of the past, but it also carries with it the promise of continuity, the assurance that we'll still be here tomorrow—eating grits. Each morning in Chapel Hill, before dawn, our friend Dip Council starts stirring the grits in her restaurant kitchen. Our invitation is to do the same, everywhere. It's a heritage all can share in. But Dip says it best: "Just put a little South in your mouth."

BASIC GRITS

. . . . . .

Basic boiled grits is the way we like to start the day, and it's the way to start this collection of recipes. In this section, you'll get the essentials of grits cooking, and then you'll get a peep into the way smart southern cooks transform leftover grits into tasty concoctions to serve all through the day.

BASIC BOILED
GRITS

Real Old South flavor and texture are found only in old-fashioned stone-ground grits. There is no other route to the deliciously rich corn flavor prized by southerners for centuries. Authentic grits are coarse in texture and require thorough cooking. Because the oily germ of the kernel is preserved under the cool grind of the stone, these grits must be consumed very soon after purchase or they will turn rancid. Luckily you can hold these grits in the freezer for up to six months.

Old recipes always direct you to first "wash" the grits. Even today most modern stone-ground grits need rinsing to separate the last remains of the hull or chaff from the kernel. Simply cover the grits with cold water. The meal will sink to the bottom, and the chaff will float to the surface where it can be skimmed off with a kitchen strainer.

> 1 cup stone-ground grits
> 4 cups water
> ½ teaspoon salt, or to taste
> 2 tablespoons unsalted butter

1. Pour the grits into a large bowl and cover with cold water. Skim off the chaff as it floats to the surface. Stir the grits about and skim again until all the chaff has been removed. Drain the grits in a sieve.

2. Bring 4 cups water to a boil in a medium-size saucepan. Add the salt and slowly stir in the grits. Cook at a simmer, stirring frequently, until the grits are done—they should be quite thick and creamy—about 40 minutes.

3. Remove the grits from the heat and stir in the butter.

Serves 4

GROCERY STORE GRITS

Most grits in the grocery store are called "quick." The corn is ground very fine and then quickly steamed. Quick grits cook in much less time than coarsely ground traditional grits, and they definitely come in handy.

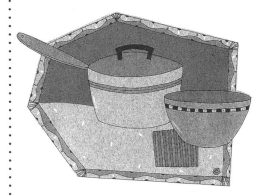

Basically the proportion of liquid to dry grits is the same (4 to 1) no matter how the grits are milled. Only the cooking time varies, and the manufacturer's directions should be followed up to a point. All instant and quick-cooking grits are improved with a longer, gentler cooking than the directions indicate. Or at the end of cooking, you can just cover the pot and let the grits swell over very low heat for 5 minutes.

CHEESE GRITS

Adding cheese is the first "company" thing we do to grits when it's time to show off a little. While Basic Boiled Grits are perfect in their simplicity for breakfast, at bigger meals Cheese Grits are more likely to appear. Cheese Grits are also the base for a number of dishes in this book. We like them topped with Spring Chicken and Grits (see Index) and as a savory base for a number of seasonal vegetarian concoctions.

1 recipe Basic Boiled Grits
    (page 22)
¼ teaspoon ground white pepper
Pinch or more of cayenne pepper
Very small grating of fresh nutmeg
1 cup shredded sharp Cheddar cheese,
    or more to taste
2 tablespoons unsalted butter
Salt to taste

Prepare the boiled grits according to the recipe. When fully cooked, remove from the heat, and add the rest of the above ingredients. Stir until smooth. Serve immediately or hold over simmering water in a double boiler up to 30 minutes.

Serves 4

EAT YOUR GRITS. THEY'RE GOOD FOR YOU.

▶ *Stone-ground grits by themselves are quite nutritious. A single serving (3 tablespoons uncooked) has only 100 calories (the same as a serving of white rice), no sodium, and no fat.*

▶ *Stone-ground grits are rich in vitamin E, which they get from the oil in the germ. Commercially processed grits are enriched with vitamins E and A and niacin to replace nutrients lost in the milling process. Instant grits provide the same nutrition as quick grits but are high in sodium.*

▶ *Grits can combine with other foods—beans, for example—to make a complete protein.*

▶ *Grits are a good source of fiber.*

▶ *There is some medical evidence that eating grits can improve your outlook on life. Serotonin, a chemical produced in the brain, plays a crucial role in a person's mood. Eating foods high in carbohydrates—for example, grits—enhances the production of serotonin.*

FRIED GRITS

Fried grits are a good way to use up any leftovers. They come to the table at lunch or suppertime but not at breakfast. Cold grits set up neatly for slicing and fry up with a deliciously golden crust.

> *1 recipe Basic Boiled Grits*
>   *(page 22)*
> *1 cup all-purpose flour*
> *¾ teaspoon salt*
> *⅛ teaspoon freshly ground black*
>   *pepper*
> *4 tablespoons (½ stick) unsalted butter*
>   *or ¼ cup fat for frying, or more if*
>   *needed*

1. Pour the hot grits into an ungreased loaf pan and let cool until quite firm, at least 30 minutes.

2. When ready to cook, invert the pan and turn out the grits. Cut into slices about ½ inch thick. Mix the flour, salt, and pepper together on a plate and dip both sides of the slices in the mixture.

3. Melt the butter in a medium-size skillet over medium-high heat. It should be about ¼ inch deep. Add the grits slices and fry until golden on the bottom, about 5 minutes. Turn and brown the second side, 5 minutes more.

Serves 4 to 6

SAUSAGE FRIED GRITS

The origin of Sausage Fried Grits may be leftover grits, but you should try it from scratch for cold-weather breakfasts and lunches. On Sunday nights after long, bone-chilling walks in the woods, we would come home to suppers like this with fried eggs, baked apples, hot biscuits, and molasses.

1 recipe Basic Boiled Grits (page 22)
½ pound Pork Sausage (recipe follows)
1 large egg
1 cup all-purpose flour
¾ teaspoon salt
⅛ teaspoon freshly ground black pepper
¼ cup oil or fat for frying, or more if needed

1. Prepare the grits and set aside.

2. Brown the sausage in a skillet over medium heat, breaking it up into small pieces as it cooks. Drain off the excess fat and stir the sausage into the grits. Beat the egg well and stir it into the grits. Pour the mixture into a loaf pan and let cool in the refrigerator or at room temperature until firm, about 2 hours.

3. Invert the pan and turn out the grits. Cut into slices ½ inch thick. Mix the flour, salt, and pepper together on a plate and dip both sides of the slices in the mixture.

4. Heat about ¼ inch oil in a medium-size skillet over medium-high heat. Add the slices and fry until golden on the bottom, about 5 minutes. Turn and brown the second side, 5 minutes more.

Serves 8 to 10

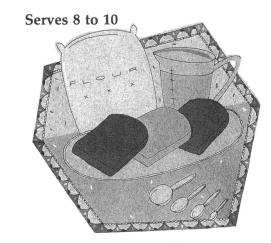

PORK SAUSAGE

Sausage in the South is most often a mixture of freshly ground pork and seasonings, the two most prominent flavors being sage and red pepper. Almost every little corner meat market grinds and seasons its own blend, and there is almost always a separate "extra-hot" batch. If that's your taste, triple (or even more) the red pepper in this recipe.

Others prize the sage and that, too, can be tripled. There is great pleasure in creating your own personal recipe; experiment with small batches and fry up a small piece for tasting. If you've made it too hot for man or beast, you can always mix in more unseasoned pork.

1 pound ground pork, not too lean
1 teaspoon salt
¾ teaspoon sugar
½ teaspoon dried red pepper flakes,
    chopped
1 teaspoon chopped fresh thyme, or ⅓
    teaspoon dried
1 teaspoon chopped fresh sage, or ⅓
    teaspoon dried
⅓ teaspoon freshly ground black
    pepper
Pinch of ground allspice

1. Mix all the ingredients together well. Refrigerate covered several hours or overnight so that the flavors can develop.

2. To cook, form the sausage meat into small patties. Place in a cold skillet, turn the heat to medium, and fry until cooked through and well browned on each side, 6 minutes per side.

Serves 4 to 6

SOUTHERN TABLE SAUCE

There are always a number of fresh vegetable condiments on southern tables in the summer.

Sometimes they are called "table sauces" because they are passed at the table—never spooned onto foods or into dishes in the kitchen—but they lack any official name. They are a lot like salsas and even serve the same purpose. They are mixed into bean and pea dishes, eaten with fried meats and seafoods, or simply relished by themselves. Some version of this sauce is usually on hand all summer. It is a wonderful early morning reminder of what season it is when you spoon it onto grits and fried eggs. As with sausage, you can add heat to your liking with more peppers. The southern hot pepper used traditionally is the long, knobby green cayenne.

2 ripe large tomatoes, chopped
½ cup chopped Vidalia or other sweet onions
½ cup chopped peeled cucumber
½ cup chopped green bell pepper
1 tablespoon minced seeded fresh cayenne or jalapeño pepper
1 tablespoon apple cider vinegar
Salt and freshly ground black pepper to taste

Combine all the ingredients in a large bowl and let sit for 15 minutes. Serve at the table from a bowl as a hearty condiment to spoon over and into grits. Store any leftovers, covered, in the refrigerator.

Makes about 2½ cups

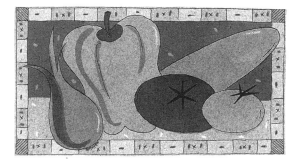

A SOUTHERN BREAKFAST

. . . . . .

The seemingly simple morning meal is the southerner's chance to display the glories of our cooking. The hams must be cured in the traditional air-dried way, the biscuits hot and steaming right out of the oven, the tomatoes just picked, and jams and jellies sharing the richness of the summer harvest. The grits will be fragrant of corn. These simple but robust country meals start off gatherings of friends and families, a send-off to the hunt or the beginning of a reunion.

A SOUTHERN BREAKFAST

BREAKFAST IN THE SOUTH

- *Boiled grits*

- *Fried country ham*

- *Red-eye gravy*

- *Boiled eggs*

- *Biscuits*

- *Jams and jellies and lots of butter*

- *Fried apples and pears*

- *Sliced garden-fresh tomatoes*

- *Hot coffee*

COUNTRY HAM

The best country hams for frying come from small butcher shops and meat markets. These survive in the South but rarely are found in the toniest neighborhoods. You will know immediately you're in the right place by the hand-lettered butcher-paper signs in the window and the sawdust on the floor. Whole hams speckled with red and black pepper should be hanging in the open air, unwrapped. We like the longest-cured hams. The test is pressing the meaty part with your thumb. Look for the least give under pressure, a sure sign that the ham is dense and intensely flavored.

2 center-cut slices, dry-cured country ham, about ¼ inch thick and weighing about 8 ounces each

1. Trim away the outer edge or rind from the ham. Cut the ham into desired serving pieces.

2. Put the slices in a cold cast-iron skillet and place over medium heat. Fry the ham gently on each side until the fat is translucent and the lean part is a deep rust red, about 10 minutes each side. Remove the ham from the skillet and keep warm until serving.

Serves 4

A SOUTHERN FAVORITE

Country hams are the salt-cured hams of Southern tradition. Water is never added and the hams are never wrapped in plastic. Both are signs of inferior modern processing. Another sure test for a country ham is the presence of a long shank. If it's there, it's the real thing. Large-scale producers remove the shank to hurry up the curing time.

RED-EYE GRAVY

Red-eye gravy is a great southern specialty and the test of many a diner or truck stop. Its slight bite and bitter flavor accents the salt and sweet of country ham and carries the flavors across the plate. Grits are the great foil for both ham and gravy; make a little depression in the grits and spoon the gravy in. Red-eye gravy is also ladled over hot split biscuits, but that's about its range.

All the rendered fat and drippings from Country Ham (recipe precedes)
1 cup hot coffee or water or a mixture of both

Into the hot skillet in which the country ham has been fried, pour the coffee or water.

Heat over medium heat, scraping up any bits that have stuck to the pan. Stir them about, but don't allow the gravy to boil. Pour it into a bowl or gravy boat and serve immediately over biscuits and grits.

Serves 3 to 4

BOILED EGGS

Boiled eggs at breakfast in the South are almost always hard cooked. This is one time to use older eggs. Very fresh eggs are poached or fried because they hold their shape better. Also, eggs for boiling must be at room temperature.

Boiled eggs are served piping hot in the shell. Peeling them takes no small amount of digital dexterity and fine motor control. Crack the egg on the edge of the plate and roll it on the table to loosen the shell. Toss the shells into a communal bowl in the middle of the table. Then split the egg, butter it, and sprinkle with salt and pepper.

8 large eggs
2 quarts water
Butter, for serving (optional)
Salt and freshly ground black pepper
   for serving

1. Let the eggs warm to room temperature. If you are in a hurry, set them in hot water for 10 minutes.

2. Bring 2 quarts water to a boil in a large saucepan. Gently lower the eggs into the water and cook uncovered at a gentle boil for 12 minutes. Drain and serve with butter (if desired) and salt and pepper.

Serves 4

FRESHLY BAKED
BISCUITS

It's hard to think of morning in the South without hot fresh biscuits. These days there are all sorts of biscuits filled with ham, sausage, steak, cheese, and chicken available from restaurants at the crack of dawn. But it really isn't difficult to do a little baking at home in the early hours. And you can rest on your laurels for the rest of the day.

- 3 cups self-rising flour, such as White Lily or Martha White
- 1 tablespoon sugar
- 3 tablespoons solid vegetable shortening, cold
- 3 tablespoons unsalted butter, cold
- 1¼ cups plus 1 tablespoon buttermilk

1. Preheat the oven to 450°F.

2. Sift the flour and sugar into a mixing bowl, and cut in the shortening and butter until the mixture resembles coarse crumbs. Quickly stir in the buttermilk.

3. Transfer the dough to a well-floured surface and knead lightly for about 20 strokes. Pat the dough into a rectangle about ½ inch thick. Cut into 2-inch rounds and place on an ungreased baking sheet. Gather up the scraps and repeat the process to make more biscuits.

4. Bake until the tops and bottoms both are golden brown, about 10 to 12 minutes.

Makes about 12 biscuits

FLOUR POWER

Southern bakers are vociferously loyal to their favorite brands of flour and with good reason. Southern flours such as White Lily and Martha White are milled from soft, low-gluten wheat which makes the lightest, most tender quick breads. "Bread" flour simply will not do at all for southern biscuits. Regular all-purpose flour may be mixed 3 parts to 1 part cake flour to approximate, but not duplicate, our special regional brands.

FRIED APPLES AND PEARS

We always have fruit for breakfast, and if it isn't this exact recipe, it's usually a variation on it. In the summer a handful of fresh berries might get tossed in at the last minute, or in the fall figs from the tree out back. Plums sliced but with the peel left on color the apples and pears beautifully. And peaches . . . .

- 3 cooking apples
- 2 slightly green Bartlett pears
- 4 tablespoons (½ stick) unsalted butter
- ¼ cup brown sugar, or to taste
- Ground cinnamon (optional)

1. Peel and core the apples and pears, then cut them into slices, about ⅓ inch thick.

2. Melt the butter in a large heavy skillet over medium heat until hot. Add the fruit and cook briskly until the slices start to brown. Reduce the heat, add brown sugar to taste, and cook until the fruit is tender and translucent but not mushy, about 10 minutes. Serve with a dash of cinnamon if desired.

Serves 4

GRITS ON THE SIDE

· · · · · ·

Grits aren't just for breakfast anymore. In our obsession with this food, we've come up with dishes that will put grits on the table anytime of the day. You'll find appetizers, snacks, fancy first courses, and a number of fine side dishes in this chapter.

CHEESE TOASTS

These hot, savory morsels are good for serving at cocktail time; they're also a nice accompaniment to soups and stews.

: *1 cup Basic Boiled Grits (page 22),*
:   *cold*
: *1 large egg*
: *1½ cups shredded sharp Cheddar*
:   *cheese*
: *3 tablespoons chopped onion*
: *2 tablespoons unsalted butter*
: *¼ cup thinly sliced Spanish olives*
: *1 teaspoon minced fresh hot*
:   *pepper*
: *Salt and freshly ground black*
:   *pepper to taste*
: *Hot sauce to taste*
: *2 tablespoons freshly grated*
:   *Parmesan cheese*
: *30 thin toast points*

1. Preheat the broiler.

2. Place the grits, egg, Cheddar cheese, onion, and butter in a food processor and run until smooth.

3. Stir the olives and hot pepper into the grits mixture. Season to taste with salt, pepper, and hot sauce. Don't be conservative.

4. Spread the mixture on the thin toasts and sprinkle the tops with Parmesan cheese. Place the toasts on a baking sheet and broil until the toasts puff and turn golden brown. Serve hot.

Makes about 30 toasts

HERBS AND SPICES

Some favorite flavors that go well with grits include:

Fresh herbs, in season: basil, thyme, chervil, parsley, chives, tarragon, and sage

Coarsely cracked black pepper

A little freshly grated nutmeg

Finely chopped roasted red peppers or jalapeños

SHRIMP AND GRITS PATE

The old southern recipes for shrimp pâté all go back to the traditional English dish of potted shrimp. It isn't surprising that the pâté is still found most often in our ancient coastal cities, such as Charleston, where time moves slowly, but still faster than change. Serve with toasts and drinks.

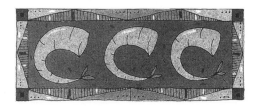

¾ pound shrimp, cooked and peeled (devein if desired)
2 teaspoons fresh lemon juice
½ teaspoon Herbsaint or Pernod liqueur
1 teaspoon Dijon mustard
6 tablespoons (¾ stick) unsalted butter, at room temperature
2 ounces cream cheese
½ cup Basic Boiled Grits (page 22), cold
¼ cup freshly grated Parmesan cheese
2 tablespoons chopped fresh parsley
¼ cup minced scallions (green onions)
Salt and ground white pepper to taste
Dash of cayenne pepper or hot sauce, or to taste
Crackers or thin toast points for serving

1. Place all the ingredients in a food processor and run until smooth, stopping the processor frequently to scrape down the sides.

2. Transfer the pâté to a bowl and chill well, at least 3 or 4 hours before serving. Serve with crackers or toast points.

Makes about 2½ cups

GRITS AND SNAILS

Cheese Grits may seem a bizarre partner for snails, but it is a combination that is as fun to serve to unsuspecting guests as it is delicious. It's surprising to us how many more folks may object to grits than to snails. This first-course dish is a sly opportunity to win converts.

SNAILS
- 1 large can snails, 24 count
- Dry white wine to cover
- ½ small onion, sliced

SAUCE
- Cooking liquid from the snails
- 1 large clove garlic, finely minced
- 3 scallions (green onions), trimmed and finely minced
- ¼ cup finely chopped fresh parsley
- 1 tablespoon finely chopped fresh chives
- 1½ teaspoons finely chopped fresh tarragon
- 6 tablespoons (¾ stick) unsalted butter, cold and cut into pieces
- Salt and ground white pepper to taste

- ½ recipe Cheese Grits (page 23), hot

1. Drain the snails and discard the liquid. Put the snails in a saucepan and cover with white wine. Add the onion and bring to a simmer over medium heat. Reduce the heat and simmer, uncovered, 15 minutes. Strain the liquid and return it to the saucepan. Discard the onion. Set the snails aside and keep warm.

2. Reduce the snail cooking liquid over high heat to about 3 tablespoons, about 7 min-

utes. Toss in the garlic, scallions, and herbs, then whisk in the butter in bits. Add the snails. Season to taste with salt and pepper.

3. Divide the grits among 4 warm plates. Spoon the snails and their sauce over top and serve immediately.

Serves 4

THE SECRET INGREDIENT

Grits and garlic have an ancient affinity in the South. Cooks who wouldn't use garlic in any other form have been slipping a bit into Cheese Grits for years. Some cooks just refer to garlic in the recipe as "the secret." These days bolder cooks can slip in a lot more garlic by roasting it first. Just put a whole head of garlic unpeeled in a tightly covered baking dish. Cook in a 350°F oven until the garlic is completely tender, about 1 hour. Squeeze the pulp out of the skins, mash, and beat into the grits.

SPINACH AND PARMESAN SOUFFLE

Souffés made with grits do without the heavy white sauce base of the more classical versions. The grits take the place of the sauce, giving both body and strength to the eggs, and the end result is less rich and fatty and more nutritious. This spinach soufflé can be prepared two or three hours ahead of time, covered, and baked at the last minute.

¾ cup freshly grated Parmesan cheese
1 pound fresh spinach
3 large eggs, separated
1 tablespoon unsalted butter
1 recipe Basic Boiled Grits (page 22),
*   cooked until very creamy*
Salt and ground white pepper to taste
Pinch of cayenne pepper
Pinch of freshly grated nutmeg

1. Preheat the oven to 350°F. Generously butter a deep 2-quart baking dish. Sprinkle the bottom and sides with 1 tablespoon of the Parmesan.

2. Rinse the spinach well. Discard all the stems and coarse leaves. Put the spinach in a pot with just the water that clings to the leaves and wilt over high heat for 3 to 4 minutes. Drain, rinse under cold water, and drain again. Press the water out of the spinach with your hands and coarsely chop.

3. Put the spinach, egg yolks, and butter in a food processor and run until mixed well but not puréed.

4. Combine the spinach mixture with the remaining Parmesan. Stir in the grits and season to taste with salt and white pepper, the cayenne, and nutmeg. Whip the egg whites until soft peaks form and fold them into the

mixture. Transfer the batter to the prepared baking dish and bake about 30 minutes. The soufflé should be nicely puffed with a gentle brown crust on top.

Serves 6

SOUFFLE PLUS
For a memorable first course or a light luncheon entrée, add a bit of any of the following to the soufflé base. Then transfer to individual buttered ramekins for baking.
Back-fin crab
Diced cooked lobster
Finely shredded country ham
Chopped cooked asparagus
Crumbled Roquefort
Diced sautéed chicken livers

CHEESE GRITS SOUFFLE

Cheese Grits Soufflé is usually served as a brunch or lunch-eon dish and is very much like a sharply flavored spoonbread.

> 1 recipe Basic Boiled Grits (page 22), made with half water and half milk
> 1 large clove garlic, crushed through a garlic press
> ½ teaspoon ground white pepper
> Dash of Tabasco sauce, or to taste
> Dash of Worcestershire sauce, or to taste
> 1½ cups shredded sharp Cheddar cheese
> ½ cup freshly grated Parmesan cheese
> 4 large eggs, separated

1. Prepare the grits. When they are fully cooked, stir in the garlic, pepper, sauces, and cheeses. Let cool slightly.

2. Preheat the oven to 350°F. Butter a deep 2-quart baking dish.

3. Beat the egg yolks lightly with a fork and stir them into the grits. Whip the egg whites until soft peaks form and fold them into the grits. Pour the batter into the prepared baking dish and bake until lightly browned and well puffed, about 30 minutes.

Serves 6

PUMPKIN GRITS

Though this dish is hardly ever seen today, it is found in the old cookbooks of the South. The combination of pumpkin and corn is also seen in old-time stews and soups and surely comes from the Native Indian cooking. You can use any of the dense winter squashes in place of the pumpkin, and canned pumpkin is a lot easier to handle than fresh. Just be sure it's plain pumpkin, not pumpkin pie filling. Pumpkin grits are especially good with ham, bacon, or sausages at breakfast.

: *1 cup puréed cooked pumpkin*
: *1 recipe Basic Boiled Grits (page 22),*
: *hot*
: *Pinch of cayenne pepper (optional)*
: *Salt to taste*
: *Unsalted butter or Red-Eye Gravy*
: *(page 31) for serving*

Beat the pumpkin into the grits. Season to taste with cayenne and salt. Serve with butter or Red-Eye Gravy.

Serves 4 to 6

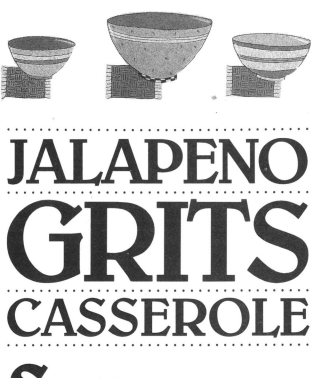

JALAPENO GRITS CASSEROLE

Some folks who won't eat grits in any other form will line up for this spicy version. It's sort of a party dish, definitely special enough for company, and it's often served at cookouts.

1 recipe Basic Boiled Grits (page 22)
2 cups shredded sharp Cheddar cheese
½ cup (1 stick) unsalted butter, cold,
    cut into pieces
3 large eggs, lightly beaten
3 tablespoons minced seeded fresh
    jalapeño or cayenne peppers
Salt and freshly ground black pepper
    to taste

1. Preheat the oven to 350°F. Generously butter a deep 2-quart baking dish.

2. Prepare the grits, add the cheese and butter, and beat until smooth. Stir in the beaten eggs and peppers and season with salt and pepper.

3. Pour the grits into the prepared baking dish. Bake until the grits are set and the top is lightly browned, about 35 minutes.

Serves 6

❝ *You tell me whar a man gits his corn pone, en I'll tell ya what his 'pinions are.*❞

—MARK TWAIN

RED HOT GRITS
Be as adventurous as your palate lets you. Stir chili powder, paprika, cayenne pepper, and ground cumin into cooked grits. Let cool, slice, and fry. Serve with black beans and salsa.

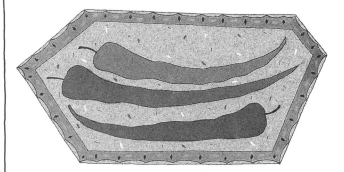

GRITS
POLENTA

Polenta is Italian for cornmeal mush. It's a great favorite these days for its affinity for full-flavored cheeses. Our dish—no surprise—is made with grits which gives a slightly coarser texture to the traditional cornmeal polenta and also a more substantial body. Since almost any word sounds better than grits, tell your picky-eating friends it's polenta first. Tell them afterwards it was grits.

1 recipe Basic Boiled Grits (page 22), hot
½ cup freshly grated Parmesan cheese
1 cup crumbled mild goat cheese, such as Bucheron
Salt to taste
2 cups Tomato Sauce (recipe follows)
¼ cup thinly sliced scallions (green onions)

1. Combine the grits, Parmesan, and ½ cup of the goat cheese in a mixing bowl. Season with the salt. Pour the mixture into a well-buttered medium-size baking dish. Let cool completely, then invert and cut into 1½-inch squares.

2. Preheat the oven to 425°F. Generously butter a medium-size baking dish.

3. Arrange the polenta squares slightly overlapping in the prepared baking dish. Spoon the tomato sauce over the polenta, but don't try to cover it evenly. Leave some areas sauceless so the polenta can toast up a little. Bake in the oven until very hot and bubbling, about 12 minutes.

4. Sprinkle the remaining ½ cup goat cheese and the scallions over the polenta. Return to the oven to just heat the cheese and scallions, about 1 minute.

Serves 4 to 6

TOMATO SAUCE

2½ tablespoons peanut oil
1 cup chopped onions
⅓ cup chopped carrot
½ cup chopped celery
2 cloves garlic, chopped
2 cans (28 ounce each) tomatoes
½ teaspoon dried thyme
½ teaspoon dried basil
½ teaspoon dried oregano
Pinch of red pepper flakes, or to taste
Salt to taste

1. Heat the oil in a large saucepan over medium-high heat. Add the onions, carrot, celery, and garlic, and cook until the vegetables are tender, about 15 minutes.

2. Add the tomatoes with their juice, and stir with a wooden spoon, breaking up the tomatoes. Add the seasonings and cook, uncovered, until the desired thickness is reached, about 1 hour. You may purée the sauce if desired.

Makes 6 to 7 cups

CORN-GRITS FRITTERS

As much as everyone talks fat-free these days, these fritters sure do travel fast out of the kitchen. In fact it's futile to try to incorporate

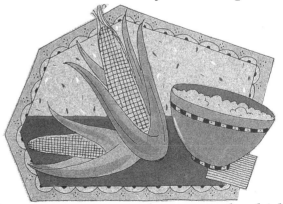

them into a menu because the kids will be circling the stove. So these fritters have become a special afternoon snack, perfect for ball game watchers. Tartar and cocktail sauces are what southerners will be looking for to dip these crisp morsels in.

1 ear fresh corn, about ½ cup corn
    kernels
1 large egg, separated
6 tablespoons milk
1 tablespoon unsalted butter,
    melted
¼ cup Basic Boiled Grits (page 22),
    cold
1 cup all-purpose flour
¾ teaspoon salt
1 teaspoon sugar
1 teaspoon baking powder
Vegetable oil or shortening
    for frying
Tartar Sauce (recipe follows)
Cocktail Sauce (recipe follows)

1. Using a paring knife, split the corn kernels down the center, then scrape them from the cob. Set aside.

2. Beat the egg yolk with the milk, butter, and grits. Or put these ingredients in a food processor and run until smooth. Stir in the corn.

3. Sift the flour, salt, sugar, and baking powder into a mixing bowl. Stir in the corn mixture.

4. Beat the egg white until stiff and fold it into the batter.

5. Pour enough oil into a medium-size skillet to reach a depth of 1 inch. Heat the oil over medium heat.

6. Drop the batter by the tablespoonful into the hot oil. Do not crowd the pan. Fry the fritters, turning once, until golden brown, about 4 minutes. Repeat with the remaining batter, adding more oil if necessary. Drain on paper towels and serve hot with tartar and cocktails sauces.

Makes about 30 fritters

FRITTERS PLUS

Fritters are a good medium for using up bits and pieces of leftovers. Any of the following may be added to the batter, alone or in combination.

½ teaspoon dried red pepper flakes
    or 1 seeded and chopped fresh
    hot pepper
Cooked shrimp or crab
Cooked artichoke heart or mush-
    rooms
Cheddar cheese cut in very small
    cubes
Shredded country ham
Chopped bell peppers
Chopped olives, green or black

TARTAR SAUCE

Tartar Sauce is the traditional accompaniment to fried foods, especially fritters or fish, in the South. Southerners love the play of sweet and tart; add sugar to your taste, but it should be there to be authentic.

- 1 cup mayonnaise
- 2 tablespoons minced dill pickle
- 2 tablespoons grated onion
- 2 tablespoons minced celery
- 1½ tablespoons chopped fresh parsley
- 2 teaspoons fresh lemon juice
- Pinch of sugar
- Pinch of ground white pepper
- Dash of Tabasco sauce, or to taste
- Dash of Worcestershire sauce, or to taste

Combine all the ingredients well in a small bowl. Let sit, covered, in the refrigerator for 1 hour before serving.

About 1¼ cups

COCKTAIL SAUCE

This is a much maligned sauce among sophisticates, but most people, fortunately, aren't that jaded. It's usually served with cold seafood—shrimp in the shell and oysters and clams on the half-shell. It's also a tangy partner for fried foods, especially fritters.

- ¾ cup chili sauce, preferably Heinz
- ¼ cup ketchup
- ¼ cup drained grated prepared horseradish
- Juice of 1 lemon
- 1 teaspoon Worcestershire sauce
- ⅛ teaspoon Tabasco sauce, or more to taste

Combine all the ingredients well in a small bowl. Let sit, covered, in the refrigerator for 15 minutes before serving. Serve cold.

About 1¼ cups

GOLDEN SCALLOPED POTATOES

This recipe was adapted from one printed on a grits package from Arrowhead Mills. This big, substantial, and gloriously golden casserole is perfect for potluck dinners in the fall and winter.

4 medium baking potatoes, peeled and very thinly sliced
9 tablespoons uncooked yellow grits
1 medium onion, finely chopped
4 tablespoons (½ stick) unsalted butter, cut into pieces
1½ cups shredded sharp Cheddar cheese
4½ cups milk, or as needed
1 teaspoon salt
Generous grinding of freshly ground black pepper (optional)

1. Preheat the oven to 350°F. Generously butter a shallow 12 × 9-inch baking dish.

2. In the prepared baking dish, make thin layers of potatoes, grits, and onion. Dot each layer with butter and sprinkle with cheese.

3. Heat the milk with the salt and pepper but do not let it come to a boil. Pour the hot milk over the potatoes; there should be just enough to cover the potatoes. Bake until the casserole is set, bubbly, and golden, about 1 hour.

Serves 6 to 8

GRITS IN THE MAIN

· · · · · ·

When it comes to grits, we'll admit we're a little fanatical. But over the years we've learned it's sometimes better to just serve up some grits than talk about them. The silent conversion is usually the lasting one. This chapter is full of opportunities for you to spread the word. Here grits take the spotlight as entrées and main dishes, the delicious focus of a meal. There are lots of vegetarian ways and suggestions here, as well as many of the traditional southern combinations of grits and seafood and meats.

MIXED MEAT MEAT LOAF

Grits give this meat loaf a smooth texture, which translates into neat and easy slicing either hot or cold. Cold, the texture is more like a French pâté.

¾ cup Basic Boiled Grits (page 22),
    cold
½ cup chopped scallions (green onions)
⅓ cup chopped celery
1 large egg
1¼ teaspoons salt
¼ teaspoon freshly ground black pepper
1 teaspoon chopped fresh parsley
1 teaspoon chopped fresh thyme, or ¼
    teaspoon dried
1 teaspoon chopped fresh oregano or
    basil, or ¼ teaspoon either dried
12 ounces ground beef
12 ounces ground pork
2 tablespoons freshly grated Parmesan
    cheese
Dash of hot sauce (optional)

1. Preheat the oven to 350°F.

2. Put the grits, scallions, celery, egg, salt, pepper, and herbs in a food processor and run just until well mixed.

3. Transfer the grits mixture to a mixing bowl and mix in the ground meats, Parmesan, and hot sauce if desired.

4. Transfer the mixture to a 9 × 5-inch loaf pan and bake until the top is brown and the juices run clear, about 45 minutes. Let the meat loaf cool for at least 10 minutes before serving.

Serves 6 to 8

LOUISIANA MEATBALLS

The Ro*tel brand tomatoes are packed in Texas and are available all over the South. They are indispensable in Cajun cooking where a sauce is often nothing more than these pepper-fired tomatoes cooked down for a few minutes. These meatballs can be served with rice, or, even better, fried grits.

1 recipe Mixed Meat Meat Loaf
  (facing page) prepared through
  step 3
½ cup all-purpose flour
¼ teaspoon salt
⅛ teaspoon freshly ground black pepper
3 tablespoons peanut oil
3 cans (10 ounces each) diced tomatoes
  with chiles (Ro*tel), or equal
  amount tomatoes with 3 tablespoons
  finely chopped fresh hot peppers

1. Shape the meat loaf mixture into small balls about the size of a cherry tomato.

2. Mix the flour, salt, and pepper together on a plate. Heat the oil in a large skillet over medium-high heat. Roll the meatballs in the flour mixture and sauté lightly until golden brown on all sides. Do not crowd the pan. Remove the meatballs from the skillet and set aside. Repeat with the remaining meat and set aside. Pour off most of the pan fat.

3. Add the tomatoes to the pan and boil rapidly for a few minutes. Return the meatballs to the pan and simmer 5 minutes.

Serves 6 to 8

GRITS AND . . .

Mustard: Dijon mustard gives grits a real kick; even better is the grainy style. To these grits with sautéed shrimp or grilled tuna.

Pesto: Wait till the last minute to stir in a bit of pesto and you'll serve up the most fragrant and delicately colored grits imaginable. Pesto grits are great fried!

Duxelles: This old warhorse of the French kitchen seems quite at home in a Southern stable. Mince mushrooms and shallots, sauté them in butter, season up, and combine with hot grits.

Tahini: Add a little of this sesame seed paste and a bit of pressed garlic for a Near Eastern plate of grits. Grilled baby eggplants brushed with fragrant olive oil and sliced tomatoes with mint and yogurt make a quick exotic meal.

GRILLADES AND

GRITS

Grillades are small, thin cutlets of beef, veal, or pork. Actually you could use chicken breasts for this recipe as well. In New Orleans, this is a robust way to start the day—it's a traditional breakfast dish for hard-working Creoles. It's also a great brunch dish, needing only a watercress salad and crusty French bread to make us think of those banana-tree-shaded patios in the Crescent City.

3 tablespoons bacon fat or lard

3 tablespoons all-purpose flour

¼ teaspoon salt

⅛ teaspoon freshly ground black pepper

1 pound thin pork loin cutlets

1 cup chopped onions

¼ cup chopped celery

½ cup chopped red or green bell pepper

1½ cups canned whole tomatoes, chopped, with juice

1 small fresh cayenne pepper, seeded and chopped, or pinch of dried red pepper flakes

1 large clove garlic, minced

About ¼ cup water

1 recipe Basic Boiled Grits (page 22), hot and liquid, but not too runny

2 teaspoons chopped fresh parsley

1. Heat the fat in a large skillet over medium-high heat. Mix the flour, salt, and pepper together on a plate. Dip both sides of the cutlets in the mixture and brown quickly on each side. Set aside.

2. Add the onions, celery, and bell pepper to the skillet and sauté until tender, about 10 minutes. Add the tomatoes, cayenne, and garlic; bring to a simmer. Thin the sauce with water, if desired. Add the sautéed pork and simmer until the pork is tender and cooked through, about 20 minutes.

3. Divide the grits among 4 warm plates. Top with the grillades and sauce. Sprinkle with the parsley and serve immediately.

Serves 4

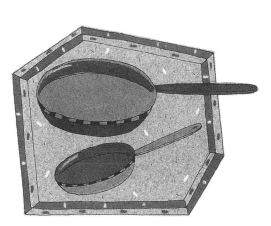

SPRING CHICKEN AND GRITS

We get our sugar snaps and scallions at the neighborly Carrboro Farmers' Market. Finding the early spring delicacies means early morning rising, but even the children don't complain for there are fried pies galore for their pleasure.

*1 pound skinless, boneless chicken
    breasts, trimmed of fat*
3 tablespoons all-purpose flour
Salt and freshly ground black pepper
2 tablespoons peanut oil
⅔ cup sliced scallions (green onions)
*1½ cups sugar snap peas, trimmed
    and stringed*
*3 tablespoons water or chicken stock or
    canned broth*
*1 large clove garlic, crushed through a
    garlic press*
*1 recipe Basic Boiled or Cheese Grits
    (page 22 or 23), hot and liquid,
    but not too runny*

1. Cut the chicken into 2-inch strips. Season the flour with salt and pepper and dust the chicken strips lightly with the mixture.

2. Heat the oil in a large skillet over medium-high heat. Add the chicken and brown lightly on all sides, 6 to 7 minutes. Remove the chicken to a warm plate.

3. Add the scallions and sugar snap peas to the skillet. Stir about until just wilted. Do not overcook. Return the chicken to the pan and add the water and garlic. Toss all about until hot.

4. Divide the grits among 4 warm plates. Spoon the chicken and vegetables over the top and serve immediately.

Serves 4

OTHER USES FOR GRITS

Like we said, grits are everywhere in the South. So it's only natural that when folks have a problem, they reach for the first thing on their shelf. To be honest, we haven't tried all of these.

1. Insecticide: Pour grits on an anthill; the ants eat the grits and disappear.

2. To stop car radiator leaks. (Well, the principle seems sound. You might want to get professional advice before trying this one.)

3. To make beer; distill the beer and you get corn whiskey, "white lightning."

4. To quiet crying babies.

5. To cure adults of dyspeptic stomach.

6. To relieve cold symptoms, make a plaster of warm (not hot) grits and apply it to the chest.

7. Warm grits make a soothing facial. Use stone-ground grits, which are rich in vitamin E.

QUAIL ON LITTLE GRITS CAKES

Almost everyone in the South knows someone who hunts, and sometimes it seems there are more who hunt game than eat it. At the least, we are offered venison, dove, squirrel, and rabbit every autumn from the overflowing freezers of our hunting friends. But the best game to our taste are the tiny quail with their rich, dark, and succulent flesh. These prized birds aren't so eagerly shared; luckily, there are good farm-raised quail in the supermarket. Like all game, quail should not be overcooked; it is very lean and dries out quickly.

GRITS CAKES
½ recipe Basic Boiled Grits (page 22), hot
½ cup sliced scallions (green onions)
¼ cup diced cooked country ham
¼ teaspoon freshly ground black pepper

QUAIL
6 quail, boned if possible*, rinsed and patted dry
Salt and freshly ground black pepper to taste
½ cup all-purpose flour
7 tablespoons unsalted butter
3 tablespoons minced shallots
½ cup very-thinly-sliced fresh white mushrooms
1 cup chicken stock or canned broth
2 tablespoons Madeira
1 teaspoon chopped fresh tarragon, or 2 teaspoons chopped fresh parsley

1. Prepare the grits cakes. When the grits are fully cooked, stir in the scallions, ham, and pepper. Pour into an 8-inch-square baking dish and let cool. When completely set, cut the grits into 2½-inch rounds and set aside.

*Ask your butcher to bone the quail for you, keeping the legs intact.

2. Sprinkle the quail with salt and pepper. Roll each in flour to coat. Melt 4 tablespoons of the butter in a medium-size skillet over medium-high heat. Add the birds and sauté until nicely browned all over, about 7 to 8 minutes. Remove the birds and keep warm.

3. Sauté the shallots and mushrooms in the pan used to cook the quail until tender, about 4 minutes. Stir in 1 tablespoon of flour (there should be enough left after coating the quail), and cook until golden. Add the chicken stock and Madeira. Cook gently 2 to 3 minutes. Return the quail to the pan with any juices they may have rendered. Add the herbs to the sauce, taste, and adjust the salt and pepper. Keep warm at the barest simmer.

4. Melt the remaining 3 tablespoons butter in a large skillet over medium-high heat. Add the grits cakes and sauté until golden, about 4 minutes on each side.

5. Place a grits cake on a warm plate. Set a quail on the cake and spoon about 3 tablespoons sauce over. Serve immediately.

Serves 6 as a first course, 3 as a main course.

SHRIMP AND GRITS

This recipe is adapted from the one first published in *Bill Neal's Southern Cooking*. When I first cre-

ated the recipe and put it on the menu at Crook's Corner, most people responded with blank stares! Then Craig Claiborne sampled Shrimp and Grits at the restaurant and immediately asked me to prepare it for him in my home the next morning. He published a glowing account of the dish in the *New York Times*, and now it is the most popular entrée at Crook's.

1 pound medium-size fresh shrimp,
  peeled (and deveined, if desired)
6 slices bacon
Peanut oil
2 cups sliced fresh white mushrooms
1 cup sliced scallions (green onions)
1 large clove garlic, crushed through a
  garlic press
4 teaspoons fresh lemon juice
Dash of Tabasco sauce
2 tablespoons chopped fresh parsley
Salt and freshly ground black pepper
  to taste
1 recipe Cheese Grits (page 23), hot

1. Rinse the shrimp and pat dry on paper towels. Set aside.

2. Dice the bacon and fry lightly in a large skillet until browned at the edges but not too crisp. Drain the bacon on paper towels and set aside.

3. Add enough oil to the fat in the skillet to make a thin layer. Heat over medium-high heat until the fat is quite hot. Add the shrimp and cook until they begin to color. Add the mushrooms and sauté, stirring frequently, about 4 minutes. Sprinkle with the scallions and bacon, then add the garlic. Season with the lemon juice, Tabasco, parsley, salt, and pepper.

4. Divide the grits among four warm plates. Spoon the shrimp mixture over top and serve immediately.

Serves 4

OPEN-FACED GRITS
Spread leftover grits in a buttered pie pan. Top with sautéed peppers, onions, and sliced sausages (Italian or chorizo). Place in a 350°F oven to heat through. Cut into wedges for a fast lunch.

SHRIMP AND CRAB LOAF

This seafood terrine is so beautiful and elegant that some will have a hard time believing it's grits at its heart. There are a number of steps, but they are all easy to execute. We usually serve this hot as an entrée, but it also makes an impressive first course, served hot or cold, with the dramatic contrast in layers. We often accompany the hot loaf with a small side of tomato sauce.

- *8 ounces shrimp, peeled and deveined*
- *1 tablespoon finely chopped onion*
- *1 teaspoon salt*
- *¼ teaspoon grated lemon zest*
- *Juice of ½ lemon*
- *1 tablespoon chopped fresh parsley*
- *Pinch of cayenne*
- *Pinch of white pepper*
- *2 large eggs*
- *¼ cup heavy (or whipping) cream*
- *2 cups Basic Boiled Grits (page 22)*
- *8 ounces fresh spinach*
- *8 ounces lump crabmeat, picked of any shell*
- *3 cups Tomato Sauce (optional; page 44)*

1. Toss the shrimp with the onion, ¾ teaspoon salt, lemon zest and juice, parsley, cayenne, and white pepper. Let marinate 20 minutes.

2. Preheat the oven to 325°F. Line a well-buttered 9 × 5-inch loaf pan with parchment paper. Butter the paper.

3. Add the eggs to the shrimp and purée in a food processor or blender until smooth. Add the cream and grits to the shrimp and process again until smooth. Transfer to a bowl, cover, and refrigerate.

4. Wash the spinach well, removing any thick stems. Place in a large pot with just the water that clings to the leaves. Cook, covered, over high heat until tender, about 4 minutes. Drain the spinach and refresh immediately under cold water. Press the water from the spinach and roughly chop.

5. Purée the spinach until smooth. Add ½ cup of the shrimp mixture and the remaining ¼ teaspoon salt to the spinach and process again until well mixed. Fold the crab gently into the spinach mixture.

6. Spread one-third of the remaining shrimp mixture in the bottom of the prepared pan, spreading it slightly up the sides. Place one-half of the spinach mixture over the shrimp leaving uncovered a slight margin of shrimp all around the sides. Add another one-third of the shrimp, then the remaining spinach, and finish with a layer of the shrimp.

7. Cover the loaf pan tightly with aluminum foil. Place in a larger baking dish and add hot water to the outer pan to a depth of 2 inches. Bake until the loaf is set and slightly puffed, about 1 hour. Remove from the oven and let sit for 10 minutes before turning out and slicing.

Serves 10 to 12 as a first course, 6 as a main course

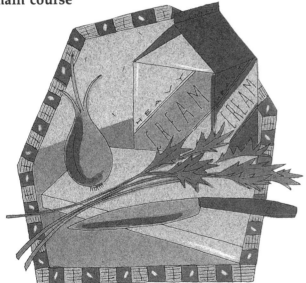

YANKEE FANS

A list of the largest metropolitan markets for grits includes New York City right along with Birmingham and Atlanta.

GRITS SHRIMP AND ARTICHOKE CASSEROLE

This is the sort of dish that good cooks all over the South used to rely on for entertaining. It may be made up a day ahead and baked off at the last minute. Today these casseroles are considered a bit old-fashioned, but everyone still asks for seconds. It's also easy to adapt the basic idea to whatever's on hand (chicken or ham, for instance), and to make it a vegetarian entrée using hard-cooked eggs when desired. Serve it with a fresh green salad.

1 recipe Cheese Grits (page 23)
3 tablespoons unsalted butter
1 small onion, chopped
1¼ cups sliced fresh white mushrooms
1 can (14 ounces) artichoke hearts
  packed in water, drained and
  quartered
2 tablespoons dry white wine
1 cup cooked peeled shrimp, or 4 hard-
  cooked eggs, peeled and sliced
2 cups White Sauce (recipe follows)
¼ cup fine dry white bread crumbs
2 tablespoons freshly grated Parmesan
  cheese
1½ tablespoons butter, melted

1. Prepare the cheese grits and pour into a buttered 12 × 9-inch baking dish.

2. Preheat the oven to 350°F.

3. Melt 3 tablespoons butter in a large skillet over medium heat. Add the onion and mushrooms and sauté until tender, about 7 minutes. Add the artichoke hearts and heat through. Pour in the wine and cook until it evaporates, 2 to 3 minutes.

4. Spoon the vegetable mixture over the grits. Sprinkle the shrimp or sliced eggs over the vegetables. Spread the white sauce over all. Mix the bread crumbs with the Parmesan and sprinkle over the white sauce. Drizzle the melted butter over the crumbs.

5. Bake the casserole until the top is lightly browned and the sauce is bubbling, about 20 minutes.

Serves 6 to 8

WHITE SAUCE

2 cups milk
1 thick slice onion
½ bay leaf
1 sprig fresh thyme
3 tablespoons unsalted butter
3 tablespoons all-purpose flour
½ teaspoon salt
Dash of hot sauce
Ground white pepper to taste

1. Steep the milk, onion, bay leaf, and thyme together in a medium-size saucepan over medium-low heat for 10 minutes. Strain and reserve the milk. Wipe out the saucepan.

2. Melt the butter in the saucepan over low heat. Add the flour and cook gently, stirring, for 5 minutes. Do not let the flour brown.

Whisk in the milk and slowly bring to a boil, stirring constantly. Season with the salt, hot sauce, and white pepper. Simmer 5 minutes more, stirring gently.

Makes 2 cups

SAVORY GRITS PIE

Here's a basic recipe for a savory custard pie that can take any number of different fillings.

Three follow; they may be stirred into the custard base or just poured directly into the pie shell. All these pies make good first courses or entrées.

> *2 cups milk*
> *3 tablespoons uncooked grits*
> *1 tablespoon unsalted butter*
> *½ teaspoon salt*
> *3 large eggs*
> *Freshly ground black pepper to taste*
> *Corn and Cheese, Mushroom, or*
> *   Shrimp Pie Filling (recipes follow)*
> *9-inch pie shell (recipe follows),*
> *   partially baked*

1. Preheat the oven to 325°F.

2. Combine the milk, grits, butter, and salt in a saucepan and cook over low heat, stirring frequently, until the grits thicken the mixture and are tender, about 15 minutes. Set aside to cool.

3. Beat the eggs vigorously with a grind or two of pepper until light. Stir them into the cooled grits mixture.

4. Spread the chosen filling in the bottom of the pie shell and pour the custard over the top. Or stir the filling into the custard and pour the mixture into the pie shell. Bake until the custard is set and the top is just lightly browned, about 35 minutes.

Serves 8 as an appetizer, 4 to 6 as an entrée

CORN AND CHEESE FILLING

: 1½ cups shredded sharp Cheddar cheese
: ¾ cup fresh corn kernels
: 1 small fresh hot pepper, seeded and
:   minced

Combine all ingredients just before using in the pie.

Makes enough for 1 pie

MUSHROOM FILLING

: 3 tablespoons unsalted butter
: 2 cups sliced fresh white mushrooms
: ¼ cup minced scallions (green onions)
: 2 teaspoons instant flour, such as
:   Wondra
: 2 anchovies, chopped
: 1 tablespoon chopped fresh parsley
: Dash of Worcestershire sauce

Melt the butter in a large skillet over medium-high heat. Add the mushrooms and sauté until most of the liquid evaporates, about 10 minutes. Add the scallions and the instant flour. Stir and cook until the mixture is dry, about 10 minutes. Remove from the heat and stir in the anchovies, parsley, and Worcestershire.

Makes enough for 1 pie

SHRIMP PIE FILLING

- 1½ cups chopped cooked shrimp
- 2 tablespoons minced scallions (green onions)
- 1 tablespoon chopped fresh parsley
- 1 tablespoon chopped fresh basil
- ¾ cup fresh corn kernels
- Dash of freshly grated nutmeg
- Pinch of cayenne pepper
- 1 tablespoon dry sherry (optional)

Combine all ingredients just before using in the pie.

Makes enough for 1 pie

PIE CRUST

- 1¼ cups all-purpose flour
- ½ teaspoon salt
- 4 tablespoons (½ stick) unsalted butter, cold, cut into pieces
- 2 tablespoons vegetable shortening, cold
- 3 to 4 tablespoons cold water

1. Sift the flour with the salt into a mixing bowl. Add the butter and the shortening. Quickly and lightly work the fat into the flour until the mixture resembles coarse crumbs.

2. Sprinkle the water over the mixture, stirring it together with a fork. Add just enough water for the dough to come together into a ball. Transfer it to a lightly floured surface and knead lightly, about 5 or 6 turns. Shape into a ball, wrap in waxed paper, and refrigerate 20 minutes.

3. Roll the dough out on a lightly floured surface to a diameter of 11 inches. Transfer the dough to a 9-inch pie pan, pressing it lightly into the bottom and sides. Moisten the edge of the dough and fold back on itself, crimping to make an attractive edge.

4. Preheat the oven to 400°F.

5. Prick the bottom and sides of the pastry with a fork. Put a double thickness of parchment or baking paper in the pie shell. Fill with dried beans or pie weights. Bake for 10 minutes. Remove the paper and the beans and return the pie shell to the oven. Bake until lightly colored, 3 to 4 minutes more. (To fully bake, continue baking 6 to 7 minutes more.)

Makes one 9-inch pie crust

EGGPLANT CREOLE

The eggplants of Louisiana are particularly delicious and abundant in the long, hot growing season. The Africans, who brought the vegetable to this country, Creoles, and Cajuns all cook with it enthusiastically. Sautéed and simmered in a piquant tomato sauce, it makes a vegetarian stew substantial enough to be a fast-day entrée.

1 pound eggplants
½ teaspoon salt
6 tablespoons peanut oil
1½ cups chopped onions
¾ cup chopped green bell pepper
¾ cup chopped celery
1 clove garlic, crushed through a
   garlic press
3 cans (10 ounces each) chopped
   tomatoes with chiles (Ro*tel), or
   equal amount tomatoes with 3
   tablespoons finely chopped fresh
   hot peppers
1 teaspoon chopped fresh thyme
Salt and freshly ground black pepper
   to taste
2 tablespoons chopped fresh
   parsley
1 recipe Basic Boiled or Cheese Grits
   (page 22 or 23), hot

1. Peel the eggplants and cut them into 1-inch cubes. Put the eggplants in a colander and sprinkle with the salt. Let drain 30 minutes.

2. Heat 2 tablespoons of the oil in a large skillet over medium heat. Add the onions, bell pepper, and celery; sauté gently until tender, about 15 minutes. Add the garlic and stir in the tomatoes and thyme. Simmer, uncovered, 15 minutes more.

3. Heat 2 tablespoons of the remaining oil in a medium-size skillet over medium-high heat. Dry the eggplant with paper towels. Add half the eggplant to the skillet and sauté gently until lightly browned on all sides and just tender, 6 to 7 minutes. Do not overbrown or the eggplant will be bitter. Transfer the cooked eggplant to the sauce and repeat with the remaining eggplant and oil.

4. Simmer all the vegetables together, uncovered, for about 15 minutes. Season with salt and pepper and stir in the parsley.

5. Divide the grits among 4 warm plates. Spoon the eggplant stew over top and serve immediately.

Serves 4

EASY CLEAN-UP

Cold grits are easier to clean up after than hot grits. Let the cooking pan cool completely and whatever is left behind will separate and pull away from the sides and bottom without sticking.

VEGETABLES AND GRITS PARMESAN

Here's a beautiful sauté of fresh vegetables spooned over grits for a vegetarian entrée. I have lots of vegetarian friends (and a vegetarian son), and I can never remember how strict they are. For vegans, who omit all egg and dairy products, use Basic Boiled Grits and have lots of cheese on the side for yourself.

When shopping for this dish, have fun. Just buy the best, most exciting vegetables. Don't take a list!

3 tablespoons olive oil

1 cup asparagus cut on the diagonal into ½-inch pieces

1 cup fresh green peas

½ cup sliced scallions (green onions)

½ cup carrots cut very thinly on the diagonal

½ cup diced red bell pepper

1 cup diced seeded peeled fresh tomatoes

2 tablespoons chopped fresh basil

Salt and freshly ground black pepper to taste

Freshly grated Parmesan cheese for serving

1 recipe Basic Boiled or Cheese Grits (page 22 or 23), hot and liquidy, but not too runny

1. Heat the oil in a large skillet over medium heat. Add the asparagus, peas, scallions, carrots, and bell pepper to the pan and stir about quickly until just tender, about 3 minutes.

2. Add the tomatoes and basil to the vegetables. Heat through thoroughly, but no more. Season with salt and pepper.

3. Divide the grits among 4 warm plates and spoon the vegetables over top. Sprinkle with Parmesan and serve immediately. Pass more Parmesan at the table.

Serves 4

STUFFED SQUASH

The old-fashioned tiny crookneck squash are what make this dish special. You will see lots of the straight yellow squash sometimes called "golden zucchini" in the market. These are watery and less tasty than our old southern squashes with necks like swans. Use these squash to accompany a roast or treat as a vegetarian entrée.

12 small crookneck yellow squash
1 cup Basic Boiled Grits (page 22),
    cold
2 tablespoons minced scallions (green
    onions)
2 large eggs, separated
¼ cup freshly grated Parmesan cheese
½ cup shredded Cheddar or mozzarella
    cheese
1½ teaspoons chopped fresh basil
Salt and freshly ground black pepper
    to taste
2 tablespoons fine dry white bread
    crumbs
1½ tablespoons unsalted butter,
    melted
2 cups Tomato Sauce (page 44)

1. Blanch the squash in boiling water until just tender, about 8 minutes. Drain and set aside.

2. Preheat the oven to 350°F. Lightly butter a 12 × 9-inch baking dish.

3. Mix the grits, scallions, egg yolks, cheese, and basil until smooth. Split each squash lengthwise and scoop out the pulp. Finely chop the pulp and beat it into the grits mixture. Season with salt and pepper.

4. Put the squash shells in the prepared baking dish. Beat the egg whites until stiff and fold them into the grits mixture. Spoon the stuffing into the shells, mounding it over the tops. Sprinkle with the bread crumbs, then drizzle with the melted butter. Bake until the filling is puffed and lightly browned, about 30 minutes. Serve with the Tomato Sauce on the side.

Serves 6 as a side dish, or 3 or 4 as an entrée

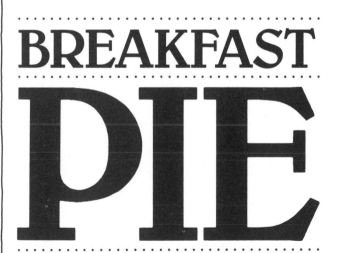

BREAKFAST PIE

Big breakfasts and brunches are great fun for everyone, especially during the holidays; for everyone, that is, but cooks like us who would rather sleep late than scramble eggs for the masses. This simple dish is our solution; it can be prepared a day ahead and baked just before serving. Adding bits of this and that, such as cooked shrimp or smoked salmon, will make you look like a genius in the kitchen while what you're really doing is cleaning out the refrigerator.

½ recipe Cheese Grits (page 23), cold
5 tablespoons unsalted butter
1 large shallot, thinly sliced
1 cup thinly-sliced fresh white
    mushrooms
1½ teaspoons instant flour, such as
    Wondra
6 large eggs
¼ cup heavy (or whipping) cream
½ teaspoon salt
⅛ teaspoon ground white pepper
2 teaspoons chopped fresh chives
½ cup shredded sharp Cheddar cheese
3 tablespoons fine dry white bread
    crumbs
½ clove garlic, crushed through a
    garlic press
1 tablespoon chopped fresh parsley

1. Preheat the oven to 350°F.

2. Place the grits in a well-buttered 9-inch pie pan and spread them to an even thickness, about ½ inch, across the bottom and up the sides of the dish.

3. Melt 4 tablespoons of the butter in a large skillet over medium heat. Add the shallot and cook until tender, 3 or 4 minutes. Add the mushrooms and continue cooking until they no longer exude liquid, about 10 minutes. Sprinkle with the instant flour and stir well.

4. Beat the eggs until foamy. Add the cream, salt, and pepper, and beat again. Stir the eggs into the mushroom mixture and cook over medium-low heat, stirring frequently until the eggs are set, 5 to 7 minutes. Add the chives and transfer the eggs to the grits shell.

5. Toss the cheese and bread crumbs with the garlic and parsley. Sprinkle over the top of the eggs. Dot with the remaining 1 tablespoon butter. Bake until hot through and the crumbs are lightly browned, about 20 minutes. To serve, cut into wedges.

Serves 4 to 6

THE MINT JULEP

A julep is just about any whiskey drink with an herb or vegetable garnish served with the intention of cooling off its consumer. In England you'll find cucumber juleps. But in the South, a mint julep is a fractious proposal. It's best to serve it with so much overbearing pride that no one else feels free to offer their own version. However we'll be so bold as to give you a starter recipe:

3 sprigs of mint, trimmed of tough stems
1 teaspoon superfine sugar (not powdered, which contains cornstarch— the corn comes later)
A silver goblet
Finely crushed ice
Bourbon
In the bottom of the goblet, crush 2 sprigs of the mint in the sugar with the back of a spoon. Fill the goblet with finely crushed ice that isn't watery. Let sit a minute until the goblet ices on the outside. Add Bourbon to taste. Aficionados do not stir. Garnish with the remaining sprig of mint.

DERBY DAY BRUNCH

The combination of fresh spring asparagus and poached eggs is a Kentucky favorite according to friends who grew up in the Blue Grass State. It seems a great way to celebrate Derby Day wherever you are.

1 recipe Cheese Grits (page 23)
4 tablespoons (½ stick) unsalted butter, at room temperature
2 teaspoons fresh lemon juice
1 tablespoon chopped fresh tarragon or parsley
¼ cup freshly grated Parmesan cheese
1 pound asparagus
Salt
1 teaspoon white vinegar
8 very fresh large eggs

1. Prepare the cheese grits and pour

them into a shallow 12 × 9-inch baking dish. Let cool until firm.

2. When the grits are firm, preheat the oven to 350°F. Lightly butter a baking sheet.

3. Cut the grits into ¾-inch-thick slices. Place 8 slices on the prepared baking sheet and heat in the oven, about 10 minutes. Keep the oven on.

4. Snap the tough ends from the asparagus. Boil briefly in a large pot of lightly salted water until just tender, but still bright green, 5 to 8 minutes, depending on their size. Drain and set aside.

5. Cream the butter and beat in the lemon juice, tarragon, and Parmesan cheese. Set aside.

6. Pour water to the depth of 2 inches

into a 10-inch skillet. Sprinkle in some salt, if desired, and add the vinegar. Bring to a boil. Crack each egg separately into a bowl and gently slip it into the water. Poach in simmering water until lightly set, 3 to 4 minutes.

7. Cover the grits slices on the baking sheet with the asparagus; then top with the poached eggs. Dab the seasoned butter over the eggs. Bake until the butter begins to melt, 4 to 5 minutes. Serve on warm plates.

Serves 4

GRITS BREADS

. . . . . .

The South is rich in baking traditions; it's a celebration of our heritage to practice it daily. Mornings are devoted to pancakes, waffles, and biscuits and an endless variety of muffins, both sweet and savory. Later in the day we bake cornbreads, spoonbreads, and yeast-raised breads. Grits are often worked into our baked goods. Thrifty southern cooks use a bit of leftover grits to create a good, crisp crust and they also add to the life of the bread.

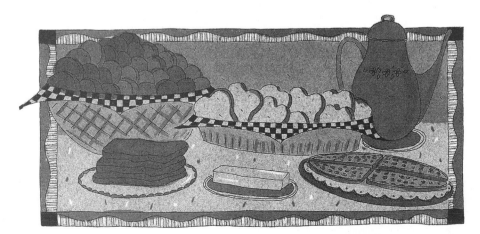

PANCAKES OR WAFFLES

This batter gets a lift from the beaten egg whites that are folded in just before cooking. The egg whites also make the pancakes more tender. You can prepare this basic batter the night before if you want to wake up to pancakes. In the morning all that's left is beating the whites, and you're ready to cook. This batter is also excellent for waffles. The high-starch and low-protein content of grits gives them a fine crisp crust. Serve both pancakes and waffles with lots of butter and maple syrup, honey, or jam.

½ cup Basic Boiled Grits (page 22), cold
2 large eggs, separated
1 cup buttermilk
3 tablespoon unsalted butter, melted
1 cup plus 2 tablespoons all-purpose flour
2 tablespoons sugar
2 teaspoons baking powder
½ teaspoon baking soda
½ teaspoon salt
Unsalted butter for cooking (optional)

1. Beat the grits with the egg yolks until smooth; then stir in the buttermilk and butter. Or place all these ingredients in a food processor and run until smooth.

2. Sift the flour, sugar, baking powder, soda, and salt together. Stir the flour mixture into the batter. (This recipe may be prepared in advance up to this point. Cover and refrigerate until ready to cook.) Beat the egg whites to soft peaks and gently fold them into the batter.

3. For pancakes, heat a griddle over medium-high heat. Lightly butter, if necessary. Drop the batter by the tablespoonful onto the griddle and cook until bubbles begin to break the surface, about 2 minutes. Turn and cook the other side until golden, about 2 minutes more. Repeat with the remaining batter.

For waffles, preheat a waffle iron. If it is not nonstick, butter it lightly. For each waffle, use about ⅓ cup batter. Close the iron and cook until the waffle is crisp and golden, 3 to 4 minutes. Repeat with the remaining batter.

Makes about 18 pancakes or 10 waffles

MORE THAN BUTTER AND SYRUP

Waffles get their name from "waba," an old German word for honeycomb. It is all those crisp little pockets that have made waffles a southern staple for centuries. And waffles show up at southern tables in more guises than is common in the rest of the country. Savory waffles are topped with crabmeat, poached eggs, and Hollandaise; creamed chicken; the spring's first asparagus; tiny game birds; fried oysters, sautéed sweetbreads and mushrooms; and on and on and on.

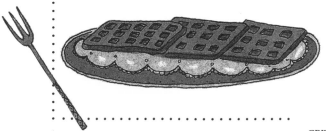

BLUEBERRY CORN PANCAKES

We make these sweet and crunchy pancakes almost all summer long: from the coastal Carolina farms' commercially grown, large blueberries in June to the last ripening of the tiny, wild mountain berries in late August. Serve them with link sausages and maple syrup.

½ cup fresh corn kernels
1 cup blueberries
1 recipe Pancakes (recipe precedes)

Combine the corn and berries and stir them into the pancake batter just before adding the beaten egg whites. Proceed as directed.

HIGH SUMMER PANCAKES

By Midsummer Night's Eve, all the early summer fruits are in, and there is no time of the year that's more exciting to the cook. Welcome the longest day of the year with these three-fruit pancakes.

- ½ cup Basic Boiled Grits (page 22), cold
- 2 large eggs, separated
- 1½ cups buttermilk
- 3 tablespoons unsalted butter, melted
- 1 cup plus 2 tablespoons all-purpose flour
- ½ cup yellow cornmeal
- 2½ tablespoons sugar
- 2½ teaspoons baking powder
- ¾ teaspoon baking soda
- ½ teaspoon salt
- ½ cup diced fresh apricots
- ½ cup blackberries
- ½ cup raspberries
- Unsalted butter for cooking (optional)

1. Beat the grits with the egg yolks until smooth, then stir in the buttermilk and butter. Or place all these ingredients in a food processor and run until smooth.

2. Sift the flour, cornmeal, sugar, baking powder, soda, and salt together. Stir the flour mixture into the batter. Gently stir in the fruits. Beat the egg whites to soft peaks and fold them into the batter.

3. Heat a griddle over medium-high heat. Drop the batter by the spoonsful onto the griddle and cook until bubbles begin to break the surface, about 2 minutes. Turn and cook the other side until golden, about 2 minutes more. Repeat with the remaining batter.

Makes about 24 pancakes

GRITS-CORN
MUFFINS

Cooked grits in the batter extends the life of quick breads like muffins. They reheat well and also toast up crisply when split.

> ½ cup Basic Boiled Grits (page 22), cold
> ½ cup cornmeal
> 2 large eggs
> 1 cup buttermilk
> 3 tablespoons unsalted butter, melted
> 1⅞ cups self-rising flour, such as White Lily or Martha White
> 1 tablespoon sugar
> ½ teaspoon baking soda

1. Preheat the oven to 400°F. Generously grease 12 muffin cups.

2. Beat the grits, cornmeal, and eggs together until completely smooth. Gradually beat in the buttermilk and butter. Or place all these ingredients in a food processor and run until smooth.

3. Sift the flour, sugar, and soda together, then gently fold it into the batter.

4. Spoon the batter into the prepared muffin cups. Bake until the tops are golden and the sides have pulled away from the pan, about 20 to 25 minutes.

Makes 12 muffins

CHEESE
MUFFINS

These savory muffins are a favorite in the winter, especially served with a hot bowl of soup on a blustery day.

: 1 recipe Grits-Corn Muffins (page 75)
: 2 tablespoons sugar
: 1¼ cups blueberries, picked over,
:   rinsed, and drained well

Prepare the batter for the muffins. Stir in the additional sugar and gently fold in the berries. Proceed as directed.

Makes 12 muffins

SAVORY MUFFINS

In your creative moments, consider adding some of the following or some inspiration of your own to a savory muffin batter. Start with ½ to ⅓ cup of any additional ingredient:

Diced country ham

Chopped black olives

Cooked seafood (crab, shrimp, or flaked fish)

Diced jalapeño peppers

Chopped sun-dried tomatoes

Fresh corn kernels cut from the cob

Sautéed chopped onion and bell pepper

BLUEBERRY GRITS MUFFINS

In June when the North Carolina blueberries start coming in, we bake these muffins every day.

: *1 recipe Grits-Corn Muffins (page 75)*
: *1 cup shredded Cheddar cheese*
: *¼ cup freshly grated Parmesan cheese*
: *Pinch of cayenne pepper (optional)*

Prepare the batter for the muffins. Gently stir in the cheese and cayenne. Proceed as directed.

Makes 12 muffins

CORN MUFFINS

It's fun to see the same recipe get a slightly different treatment and emerge as a new dish. Here we drop the corn-grits fritter batter into greased muffin tins and bake. And you can be every bit as creative in adding bits of savory morsels to these muffins as you do to the fritters. Serve alongside soup and salad at lunch.

: *1 recipe Corn-Grits Fritters (page 45)*

1. Preheat the oven to 425°F. Generously grease 12 muffin cups.

2. Prepare the batter for the fritters and spoon it into the prepared muffin cups. Bake until well puffed and brown, about 15 minutes.

Makes 12 muffins

APPLE-RAISIN MUFFINS

These deliciously moist muffins will fill the kitchen with the aromas we love most in the fall— apples and cinnamon. Like most breads made with fresh fruits, they will hold well and toast up fine the day after baking.

> Apple juice
> 1 cup raisins
> 1 medium apple, peeled, cored, and grated
> ½ cup Basic Boiled Grits (page 22), cold
> 2 large eggs
> 1¼ cups buttermilk
> 3 tablespoons unsalted butter, melted
> 2½ cups all-purpose flour
> 5 tablespoons sugar
> 4 teaspoons baking powder
> 1 teaspoon soda
> ½ teaspoon ground cinnamon

1. Preheat the oven to 400°F. Generously grease 12 muffin cups.

2. Pour enough apple juice over the raisins to just cover and let them plump a few minutes. Drain the raisins well and toss with the grated apple.

3. Beat the grits, eggs, buttermilk, and butter together until smooth. Or place all these ingredients in a food processor and run until smooth.

4. Sift the flour, 4 tablespoons of the sugar, the baking powder, and soda together and stir it quickly but gently into the batter. Stir in the fruit.

5. Spoon the batter into the prepared muffin cups. Mix the remaining 1 tablespoon sugar with the cinnamon and sprinkle it over the tops of the muffins. Bake until the tops are well browned and the sides have pulled away from the pan, 20 to 25 minutes.

Makes 12 muffins

BANANA NUT MUFFINS

These rich, flavorful muffins keep well and are a good staple to have on hand in the freezer. They are a fragrant bread for breakfast as well as for tea, and they ship well to homesick or just hungry students.

¼ cup mashed ripe banana
½ cup Basic Boiled Grits (page 22), cold
2 large eggs, separated
½ cup uncooked rolled oatmeal
1 cup buttermilk
3 tablespoons unsalted butter, melted
1⅞ cup self-rising flour, such as White Lily or Martha White
¼ cup sugar
½ teaspoon baking soda
½ cup chopped pecans
½ teaspoon orange flower water

1. Preheat the oven to 400°F. Generously grease 12 muffin cups.

2. Beat the banana and grits together until smooth. Beat in the egg yolks, oatmeal, buttermilk, and butter. Or place all these ingredients in a food processor and run until smooth.

3. Sift the flour, sugar, and baking soda together. Fold the flour mixture into the batter. Stir in the pecans and orange flower water. Beat the whites until stiff peaks form and fold them into the batter.

4. Spoon the batter into the prepared muffin cups. Bake until the tops are golden and the sides have pulled away from the pan, 20 to 25 minutes. They will smell divine.

Makes 12 muffins

BLUEBERRY GRITS COFFEE CAKE

This quick and easy coffee cake has always been a favorite for brunch at my restaurant, Crook's Corner. No one has ever guessed the secret ingredient!

TOPPING
- *¼ cup sugar*
- *½ cup chopped pecans*
- *1 tablespoon all-purpose flour*
- *2 tablespoons butter*
- *½ teaspoon ground cinnamon*

BATTER
: *8 tablespoons (1 stick) unsalted butter*
: *½ cup Basic Boiled Grits (page 22),*
: *cold*
: *½ cup sugar*
: *1 large egg*
: *1½ cups all-purpose flour*
: *1 teaspoon baking powder*
: *1 teaspoon baking soda*
: *½ teaspoon salt*
: *½ cup buttermilk*
: *1 cup fresh blueberries*

1. Prepare the topping by mixing all the ingredients together well. Set aside.

2. Preheat the oven to 375°F. Generously butter a 9-inch round cake pan.

3. Prepare the batter: Using an electric mixer, beat the butter and the grits together until light. Gradually beat in the sugar and then the egg.

4. Sift the flour, baking powder, soda, and salt together. Add the flour mixture to the batter in 3 additions, alternating with the buttermilk in 2 additions. Fold in the blueberries.

5. Pour the batter into the prepared pan. Sprinkle the topping over the cake. Bake until the topping is golden brown and a straw inserted into the middle of the cake comes out clean, about 30 minutes.

Serves 6

BLACK PEPPER CORNBREAD

This rich cornbread gets its unusual, almost creamy texture from the grits. The black pepper gives the flavor a distinct edge; use as much as your taste dictates or try substituting red pepper flakes for a change.

> *3 tablespoons unsalted butter,*
>   *melted*
> *1 cup plus 1 tablespoon cornmeal*
> *1 cup all-purpose flour*
> *1½ tablespoons sugar*
> *1 tablespoon baking powder*
> *¼ teaspoon baking soda*
> *¾ teaspoon salt*
> *½ cup Basic Boiled Grits (page 22),*
>   *cold*
> *1 large egg*
> *1⅔ cups buttermilk*
> *⅛ teaspoon freshly ground black*
>   *pepper, or more to taste*

1. Preheat the oven to 450°F.

2. Brush the sides and bottom of a 9-inch round cake pan with some of the melted butter, then dust the pan with 1 tablespoon cornmeal.

3. Sift the cornmeal, flour, sugar, baking powder, soda, and salt together. Place the remaining butter, the grits, egg, and buttermilk in a food processor and run until smooth.

Quickly but thoroughly fold the grits mixture into the flour mixture.

4. Pour the batter into the prepared pan and sprinkle the black pepper over the top. Bake until the top is slightly browned and the center is set, about 35 minutes. Let cool a few minutes in the pan, then remove the bread and cut it into wedges. Serve hot in a bread basket lined with a cloth napkin. Serve hot.

Serves 6

GREEN CORN SPOONBREAD

Spoonbread is really more a soufflé than a bread, and it is a regular part of elegant southern meals. Good cooks in both Maryland and Virginia have found through the years that it is a sublime accompaniment to the hams of the region. And every cook has a personal interpretation of this classic dish. This particular spoonbread's texture is punctuated by kernels of fresh corn.

2 cups cornmeal
6 tablespoons (¾ stick) unsalted
  butter, plus extra for serving
2½ cups water
¼ cup uncooked grits
3 large eggs, separated
2 cups milk
¼ cup all-purpose flour
1 tablespoon sugar
1 tablespoon baking powder
1½ teaspoons salt
1½ cups fresh corn kernels (about 3 ears)

1. Combine the cornmeal, 6 tablespoons butter, water, and grits in a medium-size saucepan and bring to a boil. Cook, stirring frequently, until thickened, about 5 minutes. Let cool to room temperature.

2. Preheat the oven to 450°F. Butter a 12 × 9-inch baking pan.

3. Beat the egg yolks with the milk. Sift the flour, sugar, baking powder, and salt together. Beat the egg whites to soft peaks. Stir the cut corn into the cooled batter, then stir in the egg yolk mixture. First fold in the flour mixture, then the beaten whites.

4. Pour the batter into the prepared pan. Bake until the spoonbread is puffed and just set in the middle; about 30 minutes. Do not overcook or overbrown. Serve hot with plenty of butter to melt over the top.

Serves 6 to 8

BETH TARTAN'S HOMINY BREAD

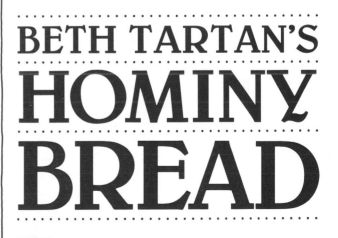

Beth Tartan is the pen name of Elizabeth Sparks who has been writing about North Carolina cooking for decades. Her specialty is the Moravian cooking of the Winston-Salem region. No one equals her knowledge and experience of the vast and rich heritage of the Southern Piedmont and mountain-area cooking. This is her recipe for a rich, spoonbread-type pudding. It is adapted from her book *North Carolina and Old Salem Cookery*.

: ½ recipe Basic Boiled Grits (page 22),
:   cold
: 1 tablespoon unsalted butter
: 1 tablespoon cornmeal
: ½ cup milk
: 3 large eggs well beaten
: Salt to taste

1. Preheat the oven to 400°F. Generously grease an 8-inch-square baking dish.

2. Mix all the ingredients together in a large bowl until smooth. Or place them in a food processor and run until smooth. Pour the batter into the prepared dish and bake until puffed, lightly browned, and set in the middle, about 35 minutes.

3. Cut into squares and serve hot.

Serves 4 to 6

GRITS BISCUITS

Good cooks in the South are thrifty cooks; they waste nothing. In fact the little bits of country ham that are saved and worked into so many dishes is one way our dishes acquire their particularly regional flavor. These grits biscuits are another example of the distinctive Southern pantry where nothing is wasted, but everything is transformed.

- *2 cups all-purpose flour*
- *2 teaspoons baking powder*
- *½ teaspoon baking soda*
- *1 teaspoon sugar*
- *1 teaspoon salt*
- *¼ cup solid vegetable shortening*
- *½ cup Basic Boiled Grits (page 22), cold*
- *¾ cup buttermilk*

1. Preheat the oven to 450°F.

2. Sift the flour, baking powder, soda, sugar, and salt into a large bowl. Cut in the shortening, blending until the mixture resembles coarse crumbs.

3. In another bowl, beat the grits with the buttermilk until smooth. Quickly stir it into the flour mixture just until mixed. Transfer the dough to a well-floured surface and knead lightly with 12 to 15 strokes.

4. Pat the dough out about ½ inch thick. Cut into 2-inch rounds and place on an ungreased baking sheet. Gather up the scraps and repeat the process to make more biscuits. Bake until lightly browned, about 10 minutes.

Makes about 12 biscuits

HEALTHY KITCHEN BISCUITS

Whole-wheat biscuits have a nutty flavor that goes well with savory additions. Try adding some chopped fresh herbs or grated cheese to the dough. A vegetarian friend of ours adds fresh sage, thyme, and red and black pepper to make meatless "sausage" biscuits.

- *1 cup whole-wheat flour*
- *1 cup all-purpose flour*
- *1 tablespoon baking powder*
- *½ teaspoon baking soda*
- *½ teaspoon salt*
- *½ cup solid vegetable shortening*
- *½ cup Basic Boiled Grits (page 22), cold*
- *¾ cup plain low-fat yogurt*
- *1 tablespoon honey*

1. Preheat the oven to 450°F.

2. Sift the flours, baking powder, soda, and salt into a large bowl. Cut in the shortening, blending until the mixture resembles coarse crumbs.

3. Combine the grits, yogurt, and honey in a food processor and run just until smooth.

4. Pour the grits mixture into the flour mixture and stir vigorously until the dough comes together and forms a ball. Transfer the dough to a well-floured surface and knead gently until the dough begins to look smooth, about 1 minute.

5. Roll or pat the dough out ¾ inch thick. Cut into 2-inch rounds and place on an ungreased baking sheet. Gather up the scraps and repeat the process to make more biscuits. Bake until golden brown, about 10 minutes.

Makes about 12 biscuits

CAROLINA GRITS
BREAD

Cooked grits have been beaten into southern bread batters and doughs for as long as there's been a South. Used discreetly, grits give breads a fine, crisp crust and strong, pully texture to the crumb. The high-starch and low-protein content of corn complements the wheat flour well.

1 package active dry yeast
1 cup plus 2 tablespoons warm
    water
Pinch of sugar
1 cup Basic Boiled Grits (page 22),
    cold
2 tablespoons vegetable oil
4 to 4½ cups all-purpose flour
1½ teaspoons salt

1. Place the yeast, 2 tablespoons water,

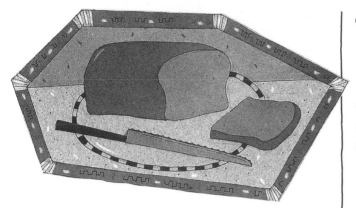

and the sugar in a large mixing bowl. Let sit until foamy, about 10 minutes.

2. Put the grits, the remaining 1 cup water, and the oil in a food processor and run until smooth. Pour the grits mixture into the proofed yeast. Add 4 cups of the flour and salt and beat hard. Transfer the dough to a work surface and knead vigorously adding more flour if necessary to prevent sticking, 8 to 10 minutes. Put the dough in a bowl, cover, and let rise in a warm place until doubled, about 1 hour.

3. Grease two 9½ × 3½-inch loaf pans with shortening and dust the bottoms and sides with cornmeal. Punch the dough down, remove it from the bowl, and knead a few minutes. Divide the dough in half, shape into loaves, and place each loaf in a prepared pan. Cover and let rise again in a warm place until

doubled, about 45 minutes.

4. Preheat the oven to 450°F.

5. Bake until the tops are golden and the kitchen smells deliciously of fresh bread, about 25 minutes. Transfer the loaves to wire racks and let cool.

Makes 2 small loaves

WHOLE-WHEAT AND GRITS BREAD

This is a great bread for sandwiches and for toasting. The grits will give it lasting power if it's kept in the refrigerator, but it usually is gone before it has a chance to reveal that attribute. The crust also develops an interesting, pebbled surface from the grits while it bakes.

: 1¾ cups warm water
: 1 cup milk
: 6 tablespoons uncooked grits
: 5 tablespoons unsalted butter
: 1 tablespoon salt
: 4 teaspoons sugar
: 1 package active dry yeast
: 2 cups whole-wheat flour
: 2½ to 3 cups all-purpose flour

1. Combine 1½ cups of the water with the milk and the grits in a medium-size saucepan. Cook over low heat, stirring frequently, until the grits swell and are tender, about 10 minutes depending on the type of grits used. Stir in the butter, salt, and sugar until dissolved. Let cool to tepid.

2. Dissolve the yeast in the remaining ¼ cup of warm water.

3. Add the yeast to the grits mixture, then stir in the whole-wheat and 2½ cups of the all-purpose flour. Transfer the dough to a well-floured work surface and knead vigorously for 8 to 10 minutes, adding more all-purpose flour to prevent sticking.

4. Butter the bottom of a large mixing bowl. Put the dough in the bowl and turn the buttered side up. Cover and let rise in a warm place until doubled, about 1 hour.

5. Grease two 9½ × 3½-inch loaf pans. Punch the dough down, turn it out of the bowl, and knead lightly for a few minutes. Divide the dough in half and shape each piece into a loaf. Place the loaves in the prepared pans, cover loosely, and let rise in a warm place until doubled, about 1 hour.

6. Preheat the oven to 375°F.

7. Slash the tops of the risen loaves several times with a very sharp knife. Bake until the tops are well-browned and the bottoms are crusty, about 35 minutes. Transfer the loaves to wire racks and let cool.

Makes two 9½ × 3½-inch loaves

FLOUR TIP
: *To substitute all-purpose flour for self-rising, to each cup of all-purpose flour add 1½ teaspoons baking powder and ⅜ teaspoon salt.*

OLD-FASHIONED CRUMPETS

This recipe goes way back. A version of it was first printed in *The Carolina Housewife* (1847), but it was already well-known and well-practiced by then. Like so many other southern dishes, this is a hybrid of European and Native American cooking. The crumpet itself is from the British Isles, but the grits are from the Indians. These little breads are great fun to make and are favored especially by children, who love to crush fresh strawberries and honey for a topping. Crumpets, like most small breads, should be split by hand, not cut.

1 cup milk
1¾ cups water
¼ cup uncooked grits
2 tablespoons unsalted butter
1 tablespoon sugar
1 package active dry yeast
3 cups all-purpose flour
1¾ teaspoons salt
½ teaspoon baking soda

1. Combine the milk, 1 cup of the water, the grits, butter, and sugar in a medium-size saucepan. Bring to a gentle boil, over medium-high heat and cook, stirring frequently, until the grits have thickened the mixture slightly, 5 minutes for quick grits, 20 or so for old-fashioned grits. Remove from the heat and let cool to room temperature.

2. Dissolve the yeast in ¼ cup of the remaining water. Sift the flour and salt to-

gether. Stir the flour into the cooled grits mixture. Add the yeast and beat hard and long (you can use an electric mixer), at least 10 minutes. The batter will still be liquid, but it should be strong and ropey. Cover and let rise in a warm place for about 1½ hours. The batter should more than double and smell yeasty.

3. Beat the batter down. Dissolve the baking soda in the remaining ½ cup water and stir it into the batter. Let rise again about 30 minutes. The batter should be very light but not doubled.

4. To cook the crumpets, grease and dust with cornmeal 12 muffin rings or tuna-can rings (see box). Place the rings on a thick griddle or cast-iron skillet preheated over medium heat. Scoop a good ⅓ cup batter into each ring. Cover the rings with a lid or a plate and cook for about 7 minutes. Remove the cover and check the crumpets; the tops should be almost set and the bottoms should be well browned. If not, cook a few more minutes before turning. Turn the rings and give the crumpets a little push so that they are in contact with the griddle. Cook until the bottoms are golden brown, about 5 more minutes. Repeat with the remaining batter. Serve fresh from the griddle or, if cold, toast before serving.

Makes about 12 large crumpets

GRITS PIZZA

Just one of the many nice things about this yeast-raised grits dough is the way it reheats. It makes a real virtue out of leftover pizza, and this crust, whether it's fresh or reheated the next day, is among the crispiest pizza crusts you'll ever bite into.

- 1 recipe Carolina Grits Bread dough
    (page 86)
- 1½ tablespoons olive oil
- 1½ to 2 cups Tomato Sauce
    (page 44)
- ½ pound shredded mozzarella
- ½ cup freshly grated Parmesan cheese,
    or to taste

1. Make the bread dough and let rise covered until doubled, about 1 hour or so.

2. Oil two 12-inch pizza or pie pans and dust with cornmeal. Transfer the dough to a floured work surface and divide it in half. Roughly and vigorously shape each half into a 12-inch round. Place each round on a prepared pan. Brush the surface of the dough very lightly with the olive oil and cover lightly. Let the dough rise in a warm place until it looks light and slightly puffy but not doubled, about 20 minutes.

3. Preheat the oven to 450°F.

4. Spread the tomato sauce over the dough and top with the mozzarella. Bake about 20 minutes. Sprinkle with Parmesan, return to the oven, and finish baking about 10 minutes more. The crust should be brown all around and the sauce bubbling hot.

Makes two 12-inch pizzas

ON TOP

Once you've got the crust down, the toppings for pizzas should reflect your own taste as well as the gifts of the season. We prefer to precook most toppings by quickly sautéeing them, but as long as it's cut thin and doesn't render too much liquid, almost any vegetable or meat will cook under the high heat a pizza calls for. Try some of these:

Eggplant
Roasted peppers
Smoked mussels
Artichoke hearts
Tuna or sardines marinated in olive oil and garlic
Fresh fennel
Chopped fresh mixed greens (spinach, escarole, or chard for starters)
Diced chicken livers
Finely shredded celery root

FRAGRANT FOCACCIA

Of course this isn't an authentic *focaccia*—the national hearth cake of Italy—but it has all the rustic and robust qualities of the original. The crust is crisp on the outside and the crumb is chewy on the inside. Your kitchen will be wonderfully perfumed with the fragrance of the Mediterranean: sharp cheese, fresh herbs, garlic, and olive oil. Serve with nothing more than a green salad.

1 recipe Carolina Grits Bread dough
    (page 86)
5½ tablespoons olive oil
8 ounces dry goat cheese, crumbled
½ cup chopped fresh herbs, such as basil,
    thyme, parsley, oregano, sage, and
    rosemary
2 large cloves garlic
8 ounces shredded mozzarella
1 cup freshly grated Parmesan cheese

1. Make the bread dough and let rise covered until doubled, about 1 hour or so.

2. Oil two 12-inch round pizza pans and dust with cornmeal. Transfer the dough to a floured work surface and divide it in half. Roughly and vigorously shape each half into a 12-inch round. Place each round on a prepared pan. Brush the surface of the dough very lightly with 1½ tablespoons of the olive oil and cover lightly. Let the dough rise in a warm place until it looks light and slightly puffy but not quite doubled, about 20 minutes.

3. Preheat the oven to 450°F.

4. Mix the goat cheese, remaining 4 tablespoons olive oil, the herbs, and garlic. Sprinkle the cheese mixture over the tops of the breads. Bake about 20 minutes. Sprinkle with the mozzarella and Parmesan, return to the oven, and finish baking about 10 more minutes. It should be beautifully golden and smell divine. Cool for a few minutes on a rack, then serve hot.

Makes two 12-inch *focacce*

HOMINY

. . . . . .

Hominy, the vegetable, is a sort of distant, elder cousin of grits and is even less known and appreciated than its cereal cousin. Outside of the South you can usually find it canned in grocery stores that cater to Black and Latin communities. It is a neutral starch that serves as a foil for stronger flavors; it also has a remarkable capacity for absorbing the richness of a simmering gravy. Here are a few recipes to encourage you to explore this staple of native American cooking.

PORK CHOPS AND HOMINY

This old southern dish develops a delicious, rich gravy as it cooks. It is even better reheated. In the South it would be served with a side of greens—turnip, mustard, or collards—and cornbread. That's a classic winter supper.

½ cup all-purpose flour
¼ teaspoon salt
⅛ teaspoon freshly ground black
    pepper
4 center-cut pork chops, ¾ inch thick
2 tablespoons peanut oil
½ cup chopped onion
½ cup sliced fresh white mushrooms
1½ cups chicken stock or canned broth
1 can (15½ ounces) hominy, rinsed
    and drained
1 teaspoon chopped fresh thyme

1. Mix the flour, salt, and pepper together on a plate. Dip both sides of the pork chops in the mixture. Heat the oil in a medium-size skillet over medium-high heat. Add the pork chops and brown on both sides until golden. Place the chops in a single layer in a 12 × 9-inch baking dish and keep warm.

2. Add the onion and mushrooms to the pan and sauté until lightly browned. Sprinkle 1½ tablespoons of the seasoned flour over the vegetables (you should have enough left) and cook, stirring, until the flour browns lightly, 3 to 4 minutes. Add the stock to the pan and bring to a boil, stirring constantly.

3. Preheat the oven to 350°F.

4. Stir the hominy and thyme into the sauce and heat through. Pour the mixture over the pork chops and bake until the chops are tender and just cooked through, about 30 minutes.

Serves 4

HOG
AND HOMINY

This is one of those dishes that's at the heart of southern cooking but is rarely tasted by outsiders. It belongs to the frost-on-the-pumpkin time of year, when the haze hangs in the valleys of the Blue Ridge until noon. Serve it for breakfast with homemade applesauce, the last and most treasured tomatoes of the season, and hot biscuits.

1 recipe Pork Sausage (page 26)
1 can (15½ ounces) hominy, rinsed
    and drained
¼ cup sliced scallions
    (green onions)

1. Shape the sausage into 8 thin patties. Place in a single layer in a cold heavy skillet and turn the heat to medium-high. Brown the patties on both sides.

2. Pour off the excess fat from the sausage. Add the hominy directly to the pan with the sausage. Throw in the scallions, cover, and heat through, 8 to 10 minutes. Thin the hominy with a little water if desired.

Serves 4

A NATIVE AMERICAN FOOD

"Saccamite" was the old creole name for hominy in New Orleans and it was brought into the city by the Native Americans to sell at their own market. Early on, the French in Louisiana established a symbiotic relationship with the natives. The young sons of early French settlers were officially encouraged to live some time observing and participating in the Native American lifestyles; much of Louisiana cooking reflects this close bond of the two cultures.

BAKED HOMINY

Baked Hominy is a Louisiana version of the dish everyone loves—macaroni and cheese.

- 2 tablespoons unsalted butter
- 2 tablespoons all-purpose flour
- 1 cup milk, heated
- 1 cup shredded Swiss or Cheddar cheese
- 1 teaspoon Worcestershire sauce, or more to taste
- Pinch of dried red pepper flakes
- Salt and ground white pepper to taste
- ½ cup of one or several of the following: diced pimientoes, sliced Spanish olives, sliced ripe olives, diced green bell pepper, or diced cured ham
- 2 cans (15½ ounces each) hominy, rinsed and drained
- 2 tablespoons fine dry white bread crumbs
- 1½ tablespoons unsalted butter, melted

1. Melt the 2 tablespoons butter in a small saucepan over medium heat. Stir in the flour and cook until golden, 8 to 10 minutes. Remove the pan from the heat and stir in the hot milk. Bring to a boil over medium heat, stirring frequently, until thickened, 6 to 8 minutes. Remove from the heat and stir in the cheese, Worcestershire, pepper flakes, salt, pepper, and one or more of the flavorings.

2. Preheat the oven to 350°F. Generously butter an 8-inch-square baking dish.

3. Stir the hominy into the sauce. Pour the hominy mixture into the prepared dish. Sprinkle the top with bread crumbs and drizzle with melted butter. Bake until the top is lightly browned, about 30 minutes.

Serves 6 to 8

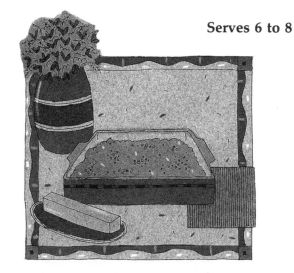

HOMINY FISH CAKES

Fish cakes are popular for breakfast throughout the entire coastal region of the South. Grouper, blues, and bass are favorite saltwater choices. Inland, these cakes might be made with catfish. Serve scrambled eggs, boiled grits, biscuits, and fresh sliced tomatoes with this recipe for a hearty waterman's meal.

- *2 slices bacon, diced*
- *¼ cup chopped onion*
- *¼ cup chopped green bell pepper*
- *1 cup rinsed, drained, and lightly mashed hominy*
- *½ cup fresh white bread crumbs, or more*
- *1 large egg, beaten*
- *1 cup flaked cooked white fish*
- *¾ teaspoon salt*
- *½ teaspoon ground white pepper*
- *3 tablespoons vegetable oil or bacon fat for frying*

1. Cook the bacon in a medium-size skillet over medium-high heat until the edges are just brown but not too crisp. Drain the bacon on paper towels and set aside. Add the onion and green pepper to the fat and cook until tender, 7 to 8 minutes.

2. Combine the onion, pepper, and bacon with the rest of the ingredients in a large mixing bowl. Taste and adjust the seasoning.

3. Form the mixture into small cakes, adding more bread crumbs cautiously if the mixture is too loose.

4. Heat the oil in a medium-size skillet and fry the cakes over medium heat until golden, about 3 minutes on each side. Drain on paper towels and serve immediately.

Serves 4

CHICKEN AND SHRIMP STEW

The South has all kinds of chicken stews that particular communities claim. The very famous Brunswick stew of Virginia is just one of many of these stews which must come originally from Native American cooking. Most reveal a base of corn (in some form) with beans. Robert Beverly, in a report on the Virginia Indians in 1705, wrote that they would "boil Fish as well as Flesh with their Homony." Our version uses all three.

1 chicken, 4½ pounds, well rinsed
2 ounces salt pork, diced
1 bay leaf
1½ cups chopped onions
¾ cup chopped celery
¾ cup chopped carrots
1 can (15½ ounces) hominy, rinsed and drained
1 cup drained chopped canned tomatoes
Pinch of dried red pepper flakes
1½ cups fresh white bread cubes
12 ounces peeled deveined shrimp
1 teaspoon Worcestershire sauce, or to taste
Salt and freshly ground black pepper to taste
4 tablespoons (½ stick) unsalted butter
3 tablespoons chopped fresh parsley

1. Put the chicken, salt pork, and bay leaf in a large pot and add just enough water to cover. Bring to a boil over medium-high heat. Reduce the heat and simmer until the

chicken is tender, about 1 hour. Remove the chicken from the stock and let cool. Discard the bay leaf. Measure the stock; you will need 6 cups. If there is too much, reduce over high heat.

2. Add the onions, celery, carrots, hominy, tomatoes, and pepper flakes to the stock. Cook over medium heat until the vegetables are tender, about 20 minutes.

3. Bone the chicken and chop the meat. Add the meat to the stock along with the bread cubes. Cook gently over medium-low heat, stirring, until the bread thickens the stew and is completely dissolved, 5 minutes.

4. Stir in the shrimp and cook until done, about 3 to 5 minutes, depending on the size of the shrimp. Add the Worcestershire and salt and pepper. Stir in the butter and parsley and serve immediately.

Serves 6 to 8

WHEN YOUR PANNED IN THE SOUTH

"Panned" is a Southern cooking term not encountered in the kitchens of the rest of the country. It means to cook something quickly over high heat in a small amount of fat. Almost anything can be panned, from Jerusalem artichokes to rabbit dipped in batter. Panned hominy is simply drained hominy tossed with hot butter.

POT O' GREENS

A pot of greens or a "mess of sallat" is basic to every southern table. The kinds of greens most often cooked are mustard, turnip, kale, and collard—and they are always well-cooked. Not over-cooked, that is, but well-cooked. It takes time to develop the flavors properly and to dispel the bitterness of many greens. A mess of greens may be a side dish, but it is just as often the focus of a meal, especially when it is prepared with a good dose of ham and hominy. This makes a complete supper, served up with cornbread and a glass of chilled buttermilk.

4 cups water
1 dried hot red pepper
½ cup chopped onion
1 pound lightly smoked ham hocks
2½ pounds greens, cleaned and picked
    over, thick stems removed
Pinch of sugar
1 can (15½ ounces) hominy, rinsed
    and drained
Salt and freshly ground black pepper
    to taste
Apple cider vinegar for serving

1. Place the water, red pepper, onion, and ham hocks in a large pot and bring to a boil. Reduce the heat and simmer, uncovered, for about 1 hour.

2. Chop the greens roughly and add them to the pot with the sugar. Simmer over gentle heat for another hour. Remove the ham hocks from the pot.

3. Pick the meat from the hocks, chop it, and return the meat to the pot. Add the hominy and cook about 10 minutes more. Add salt and pepper. Serve with a cruet of apple cider vinegar.

Serves 4

TWO-CORN CUSTARD

This custard is a substantial side dish, hearty enough to be the main course of a vegetarian dinner. Fresh herbs give it a real kick; add them to your taste.

- 2 tablespoons unsalted butter
- ½ cup chopped scallions (green onions)
- ¼ cup chopped red bell pepper
- 2 cans (15½ ounces each) hominy, rinsed and drained
- 1 can (8 ounces) cream-style corn
- 4 large eggs lightly beaten
- 1 cup milk
- ¼ teaspoon Tabasco sauce
- 1 teaspoon salt
- ½ teaspoon freshly ground black pepper
- 1 tablespoon chopped fresh basil or parsley, or more to taste

1. Preheat the oven to 350°F. Well-butter a 2-quart casserole.

2. Melt the butter in a medium-size skillet over medium heat. Add the scallions and bell pepper and sauté until just tender, about 4 minutes.

3. Add the scallion mixture to the rest of the ingredients and mix well. Pour into the prepared casserole. Bake until the custard is set, about 35 minutes. Do not overcook or let the top brown up too much. Serve hot.

Serves 6 to 8

PUMPKIN HOMINY

Pumpkin Hominy comes to us directly from Native American cooks, and it is still a popular winter dish in Louisiana. You may use chicken stock in place of the water for a richer dish, but remember that this is frontier cooking and keep it simple.

  4 cups peeled cubed pumpkin
  1 can (15½ ounces) hominy, rinsed
    and drained
  1 dried hot red pepper
  About ¾ teaspoon salt, or to taste
  3 tablespoons unsalted butter

Put the pumpkin, hominy, and red pepper in a large saucepan. Add just enough water to cover and bring to a boil. Reduce the heat, and simmer until the pumpkin is tender, about 30 minutes. Drain and add the salt, but not too much. Transfer to a warm serving dish and dot with butter.

Serves 4 to 6

GREEN BEANS AND HOMINY

This side dish is good for company since you can prepare the vegetables in advance and give them a quick reheating when you're ready to serve.

  4 tablespoons (½ stick) unsalted butter
  2 cups tender green beans, cooked
  1 cup drained rinsed hominy
  1 cup diced peeled turnips, blanched
  ¼ cup sliced scallions (green onions)
  Salt and freshly ground black pepper
    to taste

1. Melt the butter in a large skillet over medium heat. Add the beans, hominy, and turnips and cook gently for 4 to 5 minutes.

2. Add the scallions and cook another minute. Add salt and pepper and serve immediately.

Serves 4 to 6

HOMINY ROLLS

These fragrant breakfast rolls are a Chesapeake tradition. Originally, an enterprising cook must have wondered what to do with a teacup of leftover hominy and worked it into a sweet dough—a brilliant solution. These rolls are a nice little celebration in themselves.

1 cup milk
4 tablespoons (½ stick) unsalted butter
⅓ cup sugar
1 teaspoon salt
1 cup drained rinsed hominy
1 package active dry yeast
¼ cup warm water
1 large egg
Grated zest of 1 large orange
½ cup chopped candied citron
4 to 4¼ cups all-purpose flour

1. Heat the milk, butter, sugar, salt, and hominy in a medium-size saucepan over medium heat, stirring occasionally until the butter melts. Cool to lukewarm.

2. Meanwhile, place the yeast and the warm water in a large mixing bowl. Let sit to soften the yeast, 1 minute.

3. Add the hominy mixture to the yeast and beat in the egg, orange zest, and citron. Beat in enough of the flour to make a soft but not sticky dough. Continue beating very hard until the dough is slick and glossy, about 5 minutes. Put the dough in a bowl, cover, and let rise in a warm place until doubled, about 1 hour.

4. Grease well 18 muffin cups. Punch the dough down and divide it among the prepared muffin cups. Cover and let rise again in a warm place until just barely doubled, about 1 hour.

5. Preheat the oven to 400°F.

6. Bake the muffins until golden, about 18 minutes. Let cool on a wire rack 3 to 4 minutes before turning out. Serve hot with lots of butter.

Makes 18 hominy rolls

GRITS DESSERTS

. . . . . .

Linda Carman, who directs the test kitchens at Martha White Foods in Nashville, Tennessee, sends out an annual call for grits recipes in December. After rigorous testing and judging by a panel of experts, the finalists in each of several categories are presented at the World Grits Festival in St. George, South Carolina, in April. The festival celebrants vote their favorites, and the recipes are published by Martha White. You can get these prize-winning recipes or go after a prize yourself by writing Ms. Carman, in care of Martha White Foods, Inc., P.O. Box 58, Nashville, TN 37202. Here are three recipes from the Sweets category.

GRITS PUDDING

Maudene Leschinsky of Quinby, South Carolina, won in 1990 with her apple-nut pudding.

> 2 cups cooked Martha White Jim
>   Dandy Quick Grits
> 1 cup applesauce
> ½ cup brown sugar
> ¼ cup raisins
> ½ teaspoon ground cinnamon
> 1 cup Martha White BixMix
>   Buttermilk Biscuit Mix
> ⅓ cup sugar
> ¼ cup chopped nuts
> ¼ cup butter or margarine, softened
> Cinnamon Whipped Cream: 1
>   teaspoon cinnamon and 8 ounces
>   sweetened whipped cream or
>   whipped topping (optional)

Preheat the oven to 375°F. Grease a 1½-quart baking dish; set aside. Combine the grits, applesauce, brown sugar, raisins, and cinnamon in large mixing bowl. Pour into the prepared baking dish. In small mixing bowl, combine the biscuit mix, sugar, and nuts. Cut in the butter with fork or two knives until the mixture resembles coarse crumbs. Spoon over the grits. Bake 30 to 35 minutes or until browned. If serving with Cinnamon Whipped Cream, stir the cinnamon into the whipped cream or whipped topping. **Makes 4 to 6 servings**

CREAMY BUTTERSCOTCH GRITS

Eight-year-old Nicole Bulley from Columbia, South Carolina, won in the children's category with this creamy dessert.

    4 cups water
    1 cup nonfat dry milk
    1 cup Martha White Jim Dandy
        Quick Grits
    1 teaspoon salt (optional)
    ¾ cup butterscotch-flavored chips

Combine the water and nonfat dry milk in large saucepan; blend well. Bring to a boil. Stir in grits, salt, and butterscotch-flavored chips; return to boil. Cover; reduce heat to low. Cook 5 minutes, stirring occasionally. Serve warm. **Makes 6 to 8 servings**

LUSCIOUS PEACHY GRITS CHEESECAKE

Florelle Weeks, her daughter, and her granddaughter all contribute recipes to the World Grits Festival Recipe Contest. Florelle's cheesecake won her the first prize in 1989.

    2 eggs
    ⅔ cup sugar
    ½ teaspoon vanilla
    1 package (8 ounces) cream cheese
    2 cups cooked Martha White Jim
        Dandy Quick Grits (well cooled)
    1 cup (8 ounces) dairy sour cream
    1 can (20 ounces) peach pie
        filling
    2 graham cracker crusts

Combine and beat all ingredients for 10 minutes on high speed. Pour in pie crusts and bake for 25 minutes at 350°F. Raise the oven temperature to 400°F. Remove from the oven and let cool for 15 minutes. Mix together the sour cream and peach filling. Spread over the pies and return to the oven for 10 minutes. Cool before serving. **Makes 16 servings**

A GRITS LEXICON

· · · · · ·

BIG HOMINY. Whole-grain hominy after the hull has been removed.

CRACKER. Loosely, a person from Georgia. Poor whites in the Georgia hill country cracked corn in hominy blocks.

FLINT CORN. The corn that the Indians taught the early settlers to grow. The kernels are harder than that of dent corn (the type of corn which accounts for 95 percent of the corn grown in the United States; most of this is used for feed). Flint corn is ideal for grinding into grits.

GEORGIA ICE CREAM. Another name for grits.

GRITTER. Perforated metal strip used to "grittle," or grate, soft corn from the cob. The result is "grates"—coarse, moist particles either cooked in stew or mashed and fried.

HOMINY. Probably from one of several Indian terms for hulled corn, such as *ustatahamen* or *rockahominie*. In a process adopted from the Indians, the early settlers made hom-

iny by boiling dried corn kernels with lye to loosen the hulls. The resulting grains were stewed and eaten or further processed by pounding in a "hominy block," a crude mortar and pestle, to make both meal and grits.

HOMINY GRITS. Originally, grits made by drying and grinding hominy. Today the term is synonymous with corn grits.

INSTANT GRITS. Made by cooking grits and then taking the water out so that they can be reconstituted quickly with boiling water.

LITTLE HOMINY. Also called "pearl hominy," this is another name for grits.

MAIZE. Our corn (*Zea mays*). The word meant "that which sustains life" in many Indian languages. This New World grain was first encountered by European explorers in Cuba, on Columbus's first voyage. Two men dispatched to explore the interior of the island returned with a report of "a sort of grain called maize, which is very well tasted when boiled, roasted, or made into porridge."

QUICK GRITS. The grits most commonly found on grocery store shelves. In the commercial processing of grits, the germ is removed and only the starchy endosperm is ground. Quick grits are ground finer than standard grits, which are sometimes labeled old-fashioned grits, and cook in three to five minutes.

SAMP. From the Narragansett Indian word for coarse hominy or a porridge made from it.

STONE-GROUND GRITS. Grits made by grinding the whole dried kernel, the germ as well as the starchy endosperm, usually in a grist mill between a pair of burrs, or millstones. Stone-ground grits have more nutritional value and taste than commercially milled grits, but they do go rancid if not refrigerated or frozen because the oil from the germ is retained in the grits.

FINDING GRITS

. . . . . .

The folks at Martha White Foods (who make Jim Dandy Grits), Quaker Oats, and Carnation (Alber's Grits) assure us that grits are available in all fifty states, but if you live outside the South, you may have to look for them. If a store carries them, it usually shelves them with the hot cereals. In large cities, stores that cater to Blacks and other groups with southern roots are more likely to stock grits. We have also seen corn grits in the bulk food sections of some natural foods stores outside the South.

Some of the old mills that still make stone-ground grits will accept mail orders. For a price list and ordering information write or call:

The Old Mill at Guilford
1340 NC 68 North
Oak Ridge, NC 27310
(919) 643-4783

Adams Milling Company
Route 6, Box 148A
Napier Field Station
Dolthan, AL 36303
(205) 983-4233

Georgia Agrirama
P.O. Box Q
Tifton, GA 31793
(912) 386-3344

Falls Mill and Country Store
Route 1, Box 44
Belvidere, TN 37306
(615) 469-7161

INDEX

. . . . . .